The Outdoor Classroom Ages 3–7

The outdoor area is now an integral part of many early years settings and schools, but is it being used to its full potential?

This book clearly explains the learning potential of the outdoor environment and practically demonstrates how the 'outdoor classroom' can be developed in early years settings and schools. Drawing on the Forest School approach, it aims to inspire teachers and practitioners to think creatively about their outside area and how they can provide rich play opportunities for children that will further their learning regardless of any time, space or financial restraints.

Emphasizing the importance of continuity for young children, the book shows how good practice in the early years can be built on in Reception and Key Stage 1 and covers:

- what the outdoor classroom is and how it enhances children's learning;
- how experiences in the outdoor classroom can support the Early Years and Key Stage 1 curricula;
- the implications for schools using the outdoor classroom including resources, timetabling, space, parental and staff opposition;
- guidance on planning;
- activities and ideas for using the outdoor classroom.

Including practical examples and detailed case studies taken from a wide range of settings and schools, this handy text will help you to get the most out of your outside area.

Karen Constable is a reception teacher at Mark First School, UK.

Sandy Green worked within the early years sector for over 35 years, initially as a nursery nurse in both education and social services settings and later as a lecturer in further education. She is now an educational consultant and has written extensively on early years education.

The Outdoor Classroom Ages 3–7

*Using ideas from Forest Schools
to enrich learning*

Karen Constable

Edited by Sandy Green

Routledge
Taylor & Francis Group

LONDON AND NEW YORK

First published 2012
by Routledge
2 Park Square, Milton Park, Abingdon, Oxon OX14 4RN

Simultaneously published in the USA and Canada
by Routledge
711 Third Avenue, New York, NY 10017

Routledge is an imprint of the Taylor & Francis Group, an informa business

British Library Cataloguing in Publication Data
A catalogue record for this book is available from the British Library

Library of Congress Cataloging in Publication Data
Constable, Karen.
The outdoor classroom ages 3–7 : using ideas from forest schools to enrich
learning / Karen Constable.
    p. cm.
  1. Outdoor education. 2. Experiential learning. I. Title.
  LB1047.C73 2012
  371.3´84–dc23   2011048935

ISBN: 978-0-415-66724-1 (hbk)
ISBN: 978-0-415-66725-8 (pbk)
ISBN: 978-0-203-81721-6 (ebk)

Typeset in Optima
by HWA Text and Data Management

Contents

Contents

Figures

Photos

Illustrations

Preface

I played outside, where I felt the wet grass between my toes, heard the leaves rustle in the trees and witnessed a fledging bird making its maiden flight. I learnt about the weather; if it rained I got wet, if it was windy my hair blew across my face, in the sunshine I played under the trees in the cool shade.

I learnt about the sights, sounds and smells of the open air and the countryside. I explored dark, hidden corners, dug for slippery worms and chased the evasive butterflies.

I can remember those days, they are my lasting memory of childhood and they are without doubt the times that have influenced my adulthood, my career and the way I have raised my own children.

I lived in an ordinary town, in a close family group, we weren't financially well off, but my parents wanted the best start for me so I went to a school where, among other things, the outdoors was highly valued. In my early school days, many years before Forest School became a familiar phrase, I had those experiences. I took risks, climbed trees, and fell out of them; I built dens in the nearby woods, walked the local footpaths with my classmates, explored in the stream at the end of the field and learnt more about the locality than most of the adults living there.

Was I very privileged? Yes, I believe I was.

Acknowledgements

The author and publishers would like to thank the following for their cooperation and support during the process of publishing this book:

David Jessup for the use of his beautiful line drawings depicting the outdoor classroom.

The staff and children of Mark First School, for providing me with the inspiration and encouragement to write this book and for letting me include their school in this publication.

Karen Staple and the staff at Sedgemoor Manor Infants School, for sharing their Forest School with me and allowing me to include them in this book.

Claire Warden of Nature Kindergartens, for allowing me to use her kindergartens as a case study and for her support during the process of writing about her pioneering nurseries.

What is an outdoor classroom and how does it enhance children's learning?

Introduction

This book has been written to inspire you to make the most of your outdoor environment, however small and however natural or manmade the space may be. It examines some of the historical perspectives on learning outdoors and looks at how those ideas still form the basis of the experiences we offer children in nurseries and schools in the twenty-first century. You may be a parent with a boisterous three-year-old, or a teacher of an active group of Year 1 children. You might be a childminder looking for new ideas and activities, or an early years practitioner needing reassurance about your approach. Whoever you are and wherever you work, enjoy and digest the words and be inspired to offer the children in your care the best experiences and opportunities you can.

The historic perspective of outdoor learning

The theory behind using the outdoors as a learning environment is well embedded in history, starting as long ago as the late eighteenth century. The importance of children having opportunities to explore and discover freely was valued as provision that was often in direct contrast to the education taking place in mainstream schools. It began predominantly in the nursery sector, which was established as an alternative provision for young children across Europe. Some of the most important early pioneers of nursery education have placed great emphasis on the need for children to be able to visit and learn in a less structured space, developing independence and creativity.

Friedrich Froebel

It was Friedrich Froebel (1782–1852) who first began to use the term 'Kindergarten' (translated from German literally – 'garden for children'). He believed that children needed to be close to nature, making connections between themselves and the wider world in order to find and understand their place within it.

Froebel didn't want learning to be compartmentalized into specific subjects but rather an opportunity to explore how all things are linked and fit together. In his innovative nursery garden Froebel created open spaces for play alongside calmer spaces for reflection and quiet thought. The children in his care learnt to take responsibility, to care for each other and for nature through the activities and experience they could choose freely every day. Through their own self-led play and discovery the children were learning about their own place in the wider world and how they could influence their own environment.

Froebel was keen that his outdoor learning encouraged independence and creativity through investigation and discovery. Recognizing the holistic nature of a child's learning, Froebel encouraged parents to work with him and their child, accepting that education need not always be about formal learning.

Maria Montessori

Some time after Froebel, during the early twentieth century, Maria Montessori (1870–1952) was working in Rome with disabled children. It was here she began to develop ideas for a way of educating children that would remove them from, what she believed, was the overpowering grasp of teachers and parents and the formal education system in place at the time.

Once again the change in approach started through nursery provision, perhaps because many nurseries of the time were free from the restrictive regulations of the education system. Montessori provided an opportunity for children in her care to learn life skills through self-chosen activities and wanted children to explore using all their senses. She liked toys to be made of natural materials in order to help develop these necessary life skills. In her environments, outdoor play was seen as integrated with indoor, an opportunity to continue similar play but in a different environment. Montessori believed in the importance of repetition in order for the learning to become embedded, a process we now know develops new connections in the brain and supports continual growth.

It was Montessori who then went on to pioneer the concept behind linked indoor and outdoor learning, allowing children to choose where they would learn through free choice and self direction. However, the free choice was a limited choice, restricted to activities provided by the carers, and the way in which the toys and activities could be used was limited and planned for. Montessori, in direct opposition to Froebel's thinking, did not believe in learning through play, she provided experiences that were considered to be useful for life, giving the children skills of independence and decision making. Whilst Froebel had placed great importance on games, stories and imaginative play, Montessori was concerned that this led to illusion and diverted the children away from the real world.

Montessori's important decision to allow children the opportunity to roam between the inside and the outside still has great influence today, with many early years providers already creating such a space and others striving to achieve it. Reception classes are encouraged to develop this style of learning provision, but it is often unavailable for children as they progress through the following classes in Key Stage 1. There are many teachers who are now beginning to consider copying the examples set in the younger classes and who are introducing some time for these slightly older children to continue to learn through play.

Rudolph Steiner

Rudolph Steiner (1861–1925) founded his own style of education in the early years of the twentieth century in Germany, and as with so many other educators he believed it to be a good alternative to the mainstream education that was available at the time. Through his own study and observations Steiner had made a connection between the child's spirituality and their world, and wanted to develop a way of learning that allowed children to develop their cognitive and social skills in a secure and calm environment. He encouraged creative thought and self-led play, whilst allowing children to take some risks and explore their senses. The children in his care developed respect for each other and their environment and trust in their own judgements and abilities. There was great emphasis on learning important social skills and encouragement to develop good attitude to working and playing with others.

Steiner encouraged all children to use the outdoor environment and provided spaces that were as natural as possible, and included many of the elements of today's outdoor classrooms: trees, a digging area, vegetable beds, a fire pit and a composting area. There would be a covered area so that children could escape from the elements, and outside play was encouraged in all seasons regardless of the weather.

In a similar approach to that of Montessori, Steiner believed that children should learn through repetition and he therefore provided routine and familiar activities that may have been repeated daily, weekly or annually. This approach is followed and adapted by practitioners who are now following the ethos of Forest School strictly. Another element of Steiner's approach now visible in Forest School is the belief that children should be able to play without adult interference. The adult's role, he felt, was to guide and support, not to lead and teach.

Steiner education is still available today, predominantly in nursery settings, but there are some primary schools following his approach and many others who have taken elements of his theories and developed them for their own use. His style of learning is probably the closest historic model we have to our current outdoor classrooms and Forest Schools.

Outdoor learning today

These three pioneers of early education are just some of a handful whose influences can be found in our own modern education system. Despite their clear differences in style and understanding of how a child needs to learn, they all have similar desirable outcomes for the children: independence, developed decision making, social awareness and a sense of being a part of their world, rather than just onlookers. They all saw the value of the outdoors and recognized the importance of contact with nature, both wild and tamed. Children were encouraged to be risk takers and to be adventurous and to learn through active, hands-on play. It is worth noting that with the exception of Steiner, these are all nursery models, the presence of great pioneers for primary education are less prominent and certainly they do not offer the creative and imaginative ideas we have discussed for play in the outdoors.

As a nation we have moved towards more sterile and safe environments: safety matting; purpose-built, garish plastic furniture; restricted areas and limited opportunities for exploration in bland tarmac playgrounds. The movement towards introducing outdoor classrooms is beginning to address this, providing some of the opportunities that were available to the young children in the care of Froebel, Montessori and Steiner.

As a generation we have to consider whether our own anxieties about our children are actually becoming detrimental to their welfare and education. Perhaps we should learn from our predecessors and be bold enough to alter what we do now to allow a more imaginative and free flow environment, across not just the early years, but into primary education too.

The outdoor classroom – what is it?

An outdoor classroom is a space, as its name suggests, that is outside. It can be interpreted and created in a way that suits each individual establishment and the children who visit. No two outdoor classrooms will ever be the same and on each visit the environment will have changed. It doesn't have a roof, or walls. The floor may be muddy, grassy, covered in autumn leaves or new spring grass. The light is entirely from the sun and the natural, hands-on displays are interactive and ever-changing. The activities on offer can be self-chosen, adult-initiated or child-led. But quite simply it is outside.

The concept of an outdoor classroom originated in Forest School, but has evolved and whilst still remaining very much in the style of Forest School it has its own identity. Forest School, by its very name, implies that it should be in woodland, with trees and a forest floor. Of course Forest School doesn't need these conditions, however it is easy to make such assumptions and for this reason there are childcare settings and schools for whom Forest School feels like an impossibility. The outdoor classroom, however, can be anywhere outside, so regardless of the environment it feels more manageable. Forest School ethos is instilled, and similar activities and experiences can be introduced whilst the idea of increasing confidence and self-esteem are paramount.

Many outdoor classrooms in school settings are corners of their existing playing fields, small courtyards or school gardens. For many years these areas were unused, or worse still converted to playgrounds and car parks. Now with the pressure to be able to provide such provision, schools are beginning to look to their boundaries and explore the space that has been neglected for so long. The more wild and natural the area the more potential it has, but a lot can still be achieved in a more restricted and purposefully created space.

I have seen outdoor classrooms in a safely fenced area of a school field, where the children have created random paths through the undergrowth and where, in late summer, some areas become so wild and overgrown they cannot be reached. Here the children can explore freely, notice the changes in the seasons and take calculated risks. I have seen school fields with a small copse that has become a successful outdoor classroom and is visited regularly by children from all year groups. I witnessed a pre-school with a borrowed courtyard where planted tubs create the only green space, but even here the children can explore and play freely and without restriction. The one common theme is that the setting is trying to instil a sense of adventure and achievement into the children in its care. Through the origins of Forest School, praise, exploration and excitement, each has succeeded in its attempts to provide for the children.

Of course the phrase 'outdoor classroom' implies that some learning takes place there. Where the setting is, its children and their age range will determine what learning happens on each visit and how structured that learning is. As children progress through their school lives it becomes increasingly difficult to find curriculum time to allow them the freedom that the outdoor classroom requires. But working with the principle that some freedom and space is better than none, many schools are beginning to see a need for all their children, regardless of their age and perceived ability.

The nature of our education system makes the generalization that all children will learn and do well in a school environment, and whilst many thrive and enjoy their time at school, a small majority spend many of their school years feeling disillusioned and consequently they often go on to underachieve. Using the outdoors as an additional learning environment can change that perspective. It has often been noticed that the children who find classrooms threatening and scary are the same children who take charge outside and as a result they discover new skills and begin to excel.

Using the outdoor classroom introduces children to a world beyond their own back garden and it gives them time to explore and take risks in a safe environment, which in turn allows them to become more confident and self assured in all aspects of their life.

What is Forest School?

The use of the outdoor environment as a learning opportunity for young children has been increasing in the UK since the introduction of Forest School at Bridgwater College in Somerset in the early 1990s. It is becoming an integral part of many pre-school settings and in more recent years has, in response to a need for more physical play and freedom, become a part of many schools, in particular for the Foundation Stage and Key Stage 1 classes.

Forest School is a childcare concept taken from a style of provision commonly in place in rural Denmark and other Scandinavian countries. The Forest Schools active in these countries bear only a vague resemblance to the Forest Schools we have come to know in the UK. Children in these countries often spend their whole time at kindergarten outside, suitably dressed and prepared for even the coldest conditions. Many of these groups have little or no indoor space, so regardless of the extreme weather conditions these children learn and play in the outdoors. Such a free style of provision is hard to implement in the UK with the restraints of compulsory curriculum, but it is being successfully attempted in various regions and will be looked at in more detail throughout the book.

In the mid-1990s a cohort of Bridgwater College staff and early years practitioners from Somerset returned from an inspiring visit to Denmark, and set about creating their own version of the outdoor play they had witnessed. In the Early Years Children's Centre on its own campus, a new approach to learning was trialled and staff witnessed the increasing confidence and higher self-esteem in the children within their care. Even with the limitations of just a college field the children became more inquisitive and explored with increasing passion. Seeing the immediate benefits to the children in their care, they set about providing Forest School to other nurseries in the area and supporting the staff in implementing it themselves. Finding areas of woodland that were safe and secure for young children, using a college minibus and impassioning the staff, they were to begin the Forest School movement that quickly spread to other localities and it continues to grow and develop more than twenty years later.

Children were dressed in warm, waterproof clothing and encouraged to explore freely in their new surroundings. Of course there needed to be boundaries, but the children naturally chose to stay near their carers and friends, and rigorous reinforcement of strict rules was barely necessary. The children were initially taught some games and shown some experiences, but in time they began to use their new skills independently and the concept of Forest School being about the children, as individuals, began to take shape.

Within the safety of their woodland the children had a camp, with a shelter crafted from the trees of the woodland, and a fire pit, where the children gathered to warm themselves and share hot chocolate. The children learnt about staying safe by the fire, they collected wood to stoke the fire and tied bundles of small twigs to dry for future visits. They were taught to use simple tools – a saw, a pen knife – and how to tie knots to make structures and rope webs. Children were taken to the woodland once a week for the duration of their time in the nursery, starting at the age of just three years old. They went whatever the weather and both the children and the adults learnt not to complain about the cold and the wet, but to focus on the environment and what it could offer them.

Having found an initiative that was so successful the college began to share their concept with other counties and provided accredited training and advice. Visitors from all areas of education came to watch and observe Forest School in practice and they went away inspired and willing to try out the idea in their own workplaces. In the years since the first trials at Bridgwater College, Forest Schools have become an important aspect of early years education across the country. A quick Internet search brings up hundreds of results from full-time provision, to after-school and holiday clubs where the delivery of Forest School is always diverse and in keeping with their own environment and the people visiting.

Forest School as we know it now is not just about the environment – it's about the opportunity and empowerment given to the children taking part. Indeed Forest School was never just about the environment, it was always about the children. It provides a vehicle to improve self-esteem and confidence, a natural setting for children to use in order to grow and develop as people and it provides opportunities for the children to develop life-long skills and enthusiasm. Forest School has become an ethos rather than a place.

Self-esteem

In its origins, Forest School in the UK began in order to help children overcome low self-esteem and to improve their self-confidence. When it started at Bridgwater College it was a way to empower children in their environment, to develop their ability to make friends and work cooperatively. This outlook proved particularly successful with children from difficult backgrounds, with teenage students who had found school challenging and with children in nurseries learning to play and work alongside others.

Self-esteem is a measure of a person's view of themselves and their capacity to carry out tasks. It affects all aspects of our lives, makes an impact on the choices we make and the way we lead our life. Self-esteem can vary according to many factors, the task, the company and the way people speak to you, or don't speak to you. Negativity towards you and your work will affect your self-esteem, as will bullying, being asked to do something you don't understand and failing at a given task. Self-esteem is personal, no one else can measure it, but they do have the ability to alter it. There is very little doubt that children with low self-esteem find learning difficult, whereas those with a high self-esteem are more likely to thrive and do well in life.

As someone who works with and spends their daily life in the company of young children it is likely that you would expect all children to be receiving the same start in life. But as we all know sadly that doesn't happen. Some children will begin their time at nursery or school as happy, eager learners, ready to explore and find out about their world without fear. These children will know how to try things, learn by their mistakes and they will have learnt the skills of perseverance and self-control.

But whilst nurseries and schools do indeed have many children with such enthusiasm they will also have children at the other end of the learning spectrum. This second group of children may well have been disregarded by the adults in their life, with their thoughts and views ignored or not acted upon. They will be afraid of making mistakes, so they are therefore less keen to try new skills and activities. It may be that with all good intentions, rather than being neglected in their formative years they were over protected by those closest to them. This would cause the children to be wary of new experiences and to need support and guidance when exploring for themselves. This group of children is likely to have feelings of incompetence, they may not know they can do something independently and will certainly not know how to cope if things do not go according to their plan.

It would appear that in our modern world, where people rush around and where parents are likely to be working, that we are in danger of either neglecting our children's needs, or over-compensating for our lack of parent time. Either way children are growing up in a world where the parents often don't value their children's decision-making skills, where they regard wild play as too risky and as a result children spend much time at play in the indoor environment, safe from the world around them.

So why is self-esteem considered so valuable to children's learning? People with low self-esteem have a low opinion of themselves, their own ability and their own importance in life. It stands to reason that those with low self-esteem are therefore lacking in confidence as well. Such a negative outlook and a feeling of unimportance will inevitably hamper a young child's development and emotional growth. Forest School set about changing this by the development of achievable activities, where each small step is rewarded, every step of progression is praised and where the outcome is always far less important than the journey to get there. Organizing play in a way that was accessible to all who were there, the staff were able to ensure that all children received positive experiences regardless of their individual ability. Staff at the early Forest Schools were quick to acknowledge that such a positive, rewarding and rich environment met the needs of all the children.

If a low self-esteem results in lower confidence then it stands to reason that a higher self-esteem results in improved levels of confidence. Therefore by increasing a child's self-esteem you are inadvertently increasing their confidence, beginning a positive circle of development. More confidence leads to more opportunities which leads to more praise and reward, which in turn is likely to lead to increased participation and enjoyment. Children working with such a positive and happy outlook generally make good progress in all areas of their learning.

Forest School is not unique in encouraging small achievable tasks, but the environment in which children are learning and playing is less threatening than a classroom, less busy than a nursery, and has no right or wrong way of exploring. The outcome might be to collect firewood, but the journey involves seeking out the correct size stick, finding others of a similar size, collecting some string, attempting to tie a knot and storing the wood in the right place. If a child finds a stick they have achieved their first goal, if it is the desired length they have taken it a step further. On the way to completing their stick bundle the child is being praised for each small task, if they never get a whole bundle because they have been distracted by the wriggly worm under a log then they have still achieved and taken part. The next time they are asked to carry out a similar job, they know they can do it.

The adult role

The adult role in the above scenario is crucial for a good outcome. They should show an interest, even if one stick looks much like another; to that child their stick is the best. Adults should use the child's name, making praise and questions personal to them. They should crouch down and be at the child's level; talking to a grown-up's knees will never be gratifying, but seeing that adult smile, nod and laugh will bring rewards. Children who are less secure will need to know where the adults are and that they can work with them, alongside them or within sight of them, depending on their confidence. It is important to remember that initially a child is likely to be less secure in this outside environment and will probably need much encouragement at transition times, going out and coming in again, before they feel completely safe.

Children, as successful learners, are dependent on those around them and the role they play. In the outdoors there is less right and wrong and more opportunities to explore freely, which allows children to develop helpful behaviour patterns which transfer back to the classroom.

Supporting a child's behaviour

There is very little doubt among those who work with young children that self-esteem is linked to behaviour. The higher the self-esteem the more outgoing and involved the child is likely to become whilst lower self-esteem often causes frustration, upset and even anger.

Early years educators are very aware that modern media takes great delight in reminding us that the behaviour of our children is unacceptable, that there is a steady decline in the presence of good manners and politeness and that we are nurturing a generation of unruly children, soon to be teenagers and young adults. It would appear that teachers are taking the brunt of this supposed regression, not enough discipline at school and too much importance on monetary possessions often quoted as two of the biggest problems for modern day children. Using the outdoor classroom attempts to redress the balance. It has been noted time and time again that children in the outdoors behave in a different way to their indoor counterparts. Children who are classroom leaders, dominate in the playground and have a large following of friends are often not the children who cope best in the outdoors. Forest School gives the less confident, sometimes less academically talented, children the chance to shine and grow in confidence. With the emphasis being in taking part rather than achieving and being the best, the outdoor experience allows all children to achieve.

The importance of small achievable tasks is clear, all children need to know they can do something. It is irrelevant at what level they achieve, young children just want

Case study

Sarah started school with a low self-esteem. It showed itself through frustrated tantrums, answering back, screwed-up work and a frequent refusal to do the task she was offered. She was usually quiet, had problems forming friendships and spent much of her day following adults around seeking their approval.

In the early days in her reception class, Sarah was introduced to the outdoor classroom, staff knew she liked being outside and her parents reported that she spent much of her time at home playing in their large garden. On her first visit Sarah held an adult's hand for the entire session and made no attempt at all to play with the other children.

Over the next few visits Sarah started to wander further away from the adult, never far, always within sight and returning every few minutes to share some exciting news or to look at an article of interest. These return visits were always greeted with enthusiasm and praise and, feeling more important, Sarah found the courage to start sharing her finds with other children too.

Back in the classroom Sarah is by no means as confident or outgoing as the others in her class, but she is now making progress. She relishes the praise and beams when she is rewarded for her hard work. She is more likely to try a new task and it has been some time since she has torn or screwed up her drawings.

Key point

The outdoor classroom gave Sarah the freedom to move away from the adult when she felt ready and she did it in small steps seeking reassurance when she needed it. The adult praised and enthused and built up Sarah's self-esteem on every return visit and continued this excitement in the classroom. Staff are very aware that with a higher self-esteem Sarah has started to achieve and make very good progress in the classroom as well as in the outdoor environment.

to do well and take part. Because of the nature of outdoor classrooms children are encouraged to be independent in their play and to choose their own appropriate level of learning. High adult-to-child ratios ensure that the children have well-informed adults near by, ready to praise and encourage as needed. This kind of intervention is difficult in the traditional classroom set up where there is often a set outcome, with a written objective and progress that is measured by annual statistics and published results.

The benefits of a higher staff ratio and more time for talk and play are often a more focused child, a calmer approach to problem solving and more rational thinking about any problems that may arise. Children are learning how to solve their own problems, work with others and respect the decisions and ideas of those around them. In turn this leads to a reduction in conflict and in the need for adults to intervene in order to trouble shoot.

As a nation, we know that modern life brings its own stresses and complications for children as well as their parents. Parental concerns about money, status and school results can lead to a strained home life where patience and time for children may be lacking. This in turn may lead children to displaying some behavioural problems. As adults when we are put under pressure we have our own ways of dealing with such added problems to our already crowded lives. Children have not yet developed these coping mechanisms, they don't know how to change the problems for themselves and as a result they become increasingly distressed, showing us in the ways they know best. Unfortunately this may well involve hurting other children, damaging property and toys, and through displays of bad temper and frustration. It has long been accepted that children who are stressed may have some behaviour problems, have low self-esteem and lack in self-confidence. So with the knowledge that Forest School improves self-esteem and confidence, it is logical to assume that it will also help to reduce behaviour problems. By preventing some of the poor social skills often evident in young children, it is hoped that Forest School is inadvertently slowing down the numbers of young children who go on to display anti-social behaviour as teenagers and young adults.

Research into the long-term effects of Forest School is difficult to come by, but perhaps now Forest School in the UK is approaching its twentieth birthday there is scope to follow the early receivers of this approach and to accumulate information about their successive school years. It would be useful to know whether their attitude to learning remained positive and whether their improved confidence and self-esteem has had any lasting results in their school and home life. Research carried out by Knight (2009) shows quite clearly that both parents and children feel their Forest School-style experiences have helped to improve the self-esteem and confidence of the participants.

Improving attitudes to learning

Because the children having opportunities to visit Forest Schools and outdoor classrooms are predominantly choosing their own play, they become eager to learn and this helps to increase their confidence as well as their ability. A child who is learning to tie a bundle of sticks with twine, learns to cut the twine to the right length, to persevere, try different methods, possibly ask for help from another and share their strengths with other children. In all they are learning the social skills that will make them a willing and able friend in any environment. The more restrictive indoor settings are often less likely to provide such freedom of exploration and such an opportunity for perseverance and determination.

Through outdoor play even the youngest children learn important social skills: turn-taking, listening and taking part. They play independently, learn to cooperate and work together, skills that will help them as they face future challenges, both indoors and out. Children begin to learn about patience and understanding and they develop respect for their peer group and for the adults they work with.

In all good childcare settings and schools children learn that their actions can have consequences for others, good and bad, and they learn to modify their behaviour to accommodate their current location and the expectations of those around them. Given some simple, but important, rules to follow, children almost always rise to the challenge, staying within the guidelines and recognizing why they need to be there.

Case study

Christopher is in his first year at school. Despite being quite immature and having a late July birthday he began school full-time in the September after his fourth birthday. He is happy and popular and his world revolves around play and social interaction. When he is asked to join the rest of the class to listen to a story he is reluctant and works his way to the edge of the group, where he can fiddle with the toys left within reach. He is quiet and still for just a few moments before he starts to whisper to his friend and his attention is completely removed from the storytelling. He is asked to stay quiet and sit still a number of times during the story. (This will be a familiar scenario for early years practitioners and teachers of young children.)

In the outdoor classroom Christopher is busy, he doesn't return to the log circle for a drink until he is called. He plays with his friends; they build houses, make cars, chase the bears and look for the wolf's den. He is happy, noisy and completely engrossed in his activities. During the whole morning no one asks him to sit still, to be quiet or to do a task that was not of his choosing.

Key point

Christopher is busy and learning actively. The whole session is a positive experience; there is no expectation that he would do something that was not suited to him. He is keen to visit the outdoor classroom again where his behaviour is not an issue.

13

Although these are skills that can be learnt and explored in all settings, because, as previously mentioned, Forest School allows different children to shine and lead, it is inevitable that these children are also the ones learning and excelling in good social habits.

Being outdoors brings with it a new set of rules and guidelines for children to adhere to, although it should be stressed that too many rules will hinder the freedom and opportunities to explore that the children so benefit from. Children need consistency, adults who share each other's vision and agree on the level of wildness allowed in their setting and who follow the same guidelines that the children have been given.

If the rule is 'don't play with sticks longer than your arm', then however good the game is the children will need reminding about the rules. Done positively, 'that stick is rather long isn't it? Shall I help you/show you how your friend can help you safely?' the experience remains positive for all involved. The children have learnt how to stay safe, learnt a new skill and have had the rules reinforced gently. It's a far better reaction than 'put that stick down!'

Staff working in early years settings need to consider whether they are expecting too much from the children they look after and have to ensure that expectations are realistic, not just in line with what the curriculum says a child of that age should be doing, but appropriate for that child, as an individual learner. Setting realistic targets and creating learning experiences that are suitable will reduce the frustration and sometimes boredom that children feel.

Risk-taking in the outdoors

Throughout history, accidents and deaths that involve children have been newsworthy events; the rarer the accident the more reported it is. In modern times, due in some part to the escalation in methods of reporting, people are becoming increasingly aware of the dangers their children face in a modern world. This surge of information causes nervousness about child safety which in turn leads to restrictions in play for young children. It is in fact much more likely that a child will be killed in everyday life, such as on the roads or sadly in the home, than in the normal and exciting world of play and learning. However, keeping such facts in perspective with daily reporting on how dangerous the outside world can be for children is a challenge for the majority of twenty-first-century parents. Surrounded by the horrific stories of abduction, kidnap and sexual abuse, it is of little surprise that parents are anxious and cautious about where and how children play.

Perhaps the information that indoor accidents are more frequent than accidents outdoors is not published widely enough and parents are not as well-informed as they should be. Perhaps we should consider why children are more likely to be harmed inside. Is it perhaps because when children are allowed to play outside there are so many restrictions that almost all elements of risk-taking have gone. Or is it because children spend far more time indoors than out? Do modern parents consider the outside riskier and therefore set more rigid rules and more limiting boundaries? Should this fear of the world of accident and abduction be applied to the world of outdoor play?

However, there is little doubt that children need to be exposed to risk and danger in order to learn about their limitations and to learn to care for themselves. Children need to be challenged in their play and have to know how to assume responsibility for their own actions. Through this challenge children are quick to establish what their boundaries are, what they are comfortable with and how they can prevent injury to themselves. As adults we take responsibility for our own care, so it stands to reason that children need to learn to do so too.

The government regulations that limit the development of children's playgrounds and turn them into sterile and bland spaces has done little to enhance opportunities for risk-taking. Providing soft surfaces for children to fall on does little to increase their confidence, but rather more to teach children that falling doesn't hurt as much as it ought to. Many playgrounds lack the challenge of wildness and freedom, thus increasing children's curiosity about such spaces.

It is the role of adults to help keep children safe, but whilst also teaching them to develop an awareness of the dangers around them. Protecting them from all risk serves two worrying purposes: it increases a young child's curiosity about the forbidden world outside their own; and it prevents children from finding out why we are concerned for their safety. If left unanswered, children will go about finding out for themselves, which in turn can lead to the very accidents and incidents we set out to protect them from.

Modern research shows that children spend less time playing away from their home than at any other time in history. The days when children could get on their bikes and cycle off to explore the country lanes, or pay an unsupervised visit to the park are gone, and children are increasingly kept within sight of the house and accompanied by a responsible adult on even the shortest outing. Whilst adults have a responsibility to keep the children in their care safe, it is not necessary to remove all risks, and in doing so we are in danger of allowing health and safety to get in the way of the development of children's wellbeing.

It therefore stands to reason that children are less likely to know how to behave in wild environments and new situations. They are ill prepared for such challenges and perceived dangers. In fact it is likely that older children will seek their risks and thrills inappropriately, sending them outside the safe boundaries we have created.

Using an outdoor classroom regularly will give children an opportunity to take some risks in everyday life. We are not talking about using a chainsaw to fell a tree or swinging on a poorly tied rope swing, but about safe fire-building, using some simple hand tools and learning to solve problems with care. Adults working in the outdoors need to be well trained, relaxed and united in their approach to risk and safety. Children are very quick to notice whether these adults are anxious and, whether intentional or not, an over-anxious member of staff will pass their concerns to the children in their care. Consider the consequences of the child taking that risk, is it really dangerous, or more likely that the child will come away unscathed, or with a bruise or minor scratch?

Case study

Peter was a lively little seven-year-old, who was well known for his adventurous spirit and his frequent attempts to break the rules and push the boundaries.

Staff at his school were aware that at home he frequently made his own rather wild play, with very few limits on his behaviour. At school he liked to cause a disruption to the work going on in his classroom, turning over a chair or running from the room several times throughout the day. It was felt this behaviour was an attempt to get some attention and it usually worked!

Whilst working in the outdoor classroom he usually behaved in a more acceptable way, but he would occasionally try to climb one of the forbidden trees. The more the teacher tried to intervene, the more likely it was he would climb to a point in the tree just beyond the safe grasp of an adult.

In response to his erratic and unsafe behaviour the teacher took a large PE mat down to the storage shed and when Peter climbed the tree the mat was placed underneath and the other children were taken to a different area. One member of staff always remained within sight of Peter. Eventually he started climbing down on his own to find out what the others were doing, and as the year progressed the tree climbing became less frequent and less disruptive.

Key point

Peter was looking for attention, when he received none for his rule breaking he stopped doing it. The teacher was determined that the behaviour of one child would not stop the class from accessing this important part of her curriculum. With the cooperation of the head teacher, an extra member of staff was allocated for the visits to the outside. The presence of the extra adult and the placement of a safety mat ensured that Peter remained safe until he had worked through his problems.

Practitioners should know when to intervene according to the child's individual needs, whilst still allowing freedom for exploring within the safe boundaries agreed by all. They should celebrate achievement and praise sensible decision making, treat children with respect, teaching them to control their own risk through suitable opportunities. Carers with a positive attitude will be teaching children to have a go, try again and persevere in their endeavours.

Importantly boys and girls must be given equal opportunities; whilst it is still believed by some that boys climb trees and girls do not, it must be understood that all children are different and should be given experiences that challenge them regardless of gender. Of course, there will always be a few children for whom boundaries are there to be pushed and risks to be fully explored with little concern for their own safety or that of those around them. This is where the adult should lead by example, share these experiences with the children and help the children make their own assessment about what they consider safe. It should never be considered fair that all children have their boundaries restricted because of the behaviour of the minority.

Children need to learn that getting hurt, stung or falling over is a part of play, and the small cuts and bruises that come from such incidents are a natural part of finding out. No manner of health and safety guidelines can prevent children tripping or running into each other and the vast majority of children suffer no ill effects from such incidents. Such an attitude should now be applied to playing and taking risks in a wild environment such as the outdoor classroom.

The benefits of taking some risks will usually far outweigh the dangers, and through this children are given a sense of independence, freedom and choice. They learn to make decisions based on their own opinions without intervention from adults; they work with others, share ideas. Children grow in confidence, develop a sense of trust of each other and learn through their own mistakes. Children learn to use tools with safety and care; they grow stronger and braver, share their experiences with others and develop into sensible explorers.

Improving health and physical development through outdoor play

It is well researched, documented and reported that, as we progress through the modern age, children are becoming increasingly more likely to be obese. A Department of Health study carried out in 2006 stated that 30 per cent of children between the ages of two and ten are classed as obese. The study looked particularly at children from poorer backgrounds and those in inner cities where the problem of obesity in children is more widespread. This may be accounted for by the lack of safe green spaces in which children can play unsupervised in our inner cities. It may be a factor of modern life, where often both parents are forced to work full-time in order to maintain the standard of living they want, that children are sent to day care where play is supervised and often restricted. Perhaps it is because with all the modern technology available to children that they no longer seek the excitement of the wild outdoors. It is most likely a combination of all of these, and our role is now to reintroduce the excitement of unplanned and evolving play experiences to these modern-day children.

The 1990s project carried out by the University of Bristol has published its findings about eleven-year-olds and their levels of activity (Banks, Hamilton Shield & Sharp, 2011). The authors suggest that their research carried out in 2003/4 has found that less than three per cent of eleven-year-old children in the UK have the recommended amount of exercise daily. In fact in some cases it is significantly less than the suggested 60 minutes of vigorous play. It would be interesting to follow some of the children who access outdoor play frequently into their later childhood in order to monitor whether their activity levels remain higher.

Whilst it is clear that diet plays a big part in the issue of obesity, it is also apparent that children have less opportunity for physical exercise than in previous generations. Children are taken to organized sports events for a limited time, they are given the required amount of physical exercise at school and many children do indeed have opportunities for supervised outside play. However, it would appear that there are many children for whom exercise is not important, for whom these opportunities are either not available or not actively encouraged. What they do seem to have a lack of is the opportunity for free play and exploration in the wider world.

Obesity in children is known to cause serious and life-threatening health issues, such as diabetes and cardiovascular disease, but it is less documented that obesity can cause psychological illness as well. Overweight children are prone to suffer from all the same worries and concerns as overweight adults. They are likely to have a low self-esteem, caused by their interpretation of their self-worth and their value to society; in turn this often leads to a lack of confidence. Children suffering from obesity are more likely than their peers to be bullied and discriminated against because of their size. It all paints a very bleak picture for our children. As teachers and practitioners, we have a duty to counteract any bad habits being formed at home, by encouraging parental involvement in any process that helps to improve the child's outlook. Forest School and the use of an outdoor classroom will help to reinstate the child's confidence, and if developed into a countrywide initiative it may help to minimize future problems.

Bad lifestyle habits developed in childhood can become a problem as children develop into adults. A culture of being indoors and using cars to get around every day is now widespread, and young adults are accepting that this is the way in which they should behave. Knowing that overweight children are likely to become overweight adults should be the inspiration behind encouraging youngsters to partake in more regular physical activity. Forest School and outdoor play fosters a love of the environment and it is hoped that such a regular intervention will change the way children perceive exercise as they grow up.

As discussed, Forest School and the outdoor classroom can help to address this modern-day problem of unhealthy lifestyles by allowing children more space in which to move and explore. It shows children that exercise does not have to be organized, indoor or adult-led sport, but rather fun, free and initiated by the children themselves.

The Early Years Foundation Stage curriculum (EYFS) makes clear links to a child's physical development, placing equal importance on fine and gross motor skills. In the outdoor classroom young children can learn to move with caution, taking note

Case study

There was a fallen tree across the path in the outdoor classroom. It had been there for a number of years and had undergrowth growing around it. Children crossed it in many ways; some used their hands for support as they put one leg over then the other. Others would climb on top and jump off, and one or two more confident children took a run at it and jumped right over. After some strong winds a second tree had fallen over the same path, which staff noted completely changed the way the children approached it. The second tree was covered in ivy and the tree trunk was barely visible. Some children tackled it with confidence using skills learnt on the first tree, most were a little more cautious. One child in particular was approaching the tree, looking at it, watching the other children, then turning around and returning the way he had come. He did this several times.

Later that same session he was back at the tree with an adult who helped him over the first time and supported him when he wanted to go back. The child spent the rest of the morning independently crossing the tree in various ways.

Key points

Unplanned activities often provide a new challenge for children; in this case it was a fallen tree that gave a new dimension to the way this child thought about his own ability. Carefully considering the new challenge the boy lacked the confidence to attempt to climb over it. After just a few moments of being helped with a sensitive adult he realized that he could take on the task and he enjoyed exploring the new obstacle independently for the rest of the session. During the morning that child leant that his skills were transferable; he found out that he had the ability to take on a different challenge, he just needed someone skilled to show him.

of and managing the uneven surfaces and obstacles around them. Opportunities for climbing, crawling, balancing and generally improving their coordination are readily available without the need to plan for them. However the practitioner can develop these experiences through personalized planning and through the support offered by well informed adults.

Challenges such as the above are difficult to replicate in a classroom or even in a normal school playground without being planned for and set up by an adult.

Case study

Tariq was a clumsy five-year-old in his first year at school. His large movements were awkward and when he was excited he would stumble occasionally. However it was his fine motor skills that were of concern to the staff in his classroom; he had difficulty holding a pencil and was not sure which hand he favoured. He would use his fingers to eat rather than use the knife and fork, and when unable to use his finger and thumb he would just take a fistful. All the attention was aimed at improving Tariq's fine motor control.

When he started to use the outdoor classroom it quickly became very apparent that his gross motor skills also needed some development. Faced with uneven ground, mud, fallen branches and tall undergrowth, Tariq would fall and trip. He was very cautious about entering new and challenging spaces. Without these visits to the outdoor classroom this issue may not have been apparent to the staff. Following observation Tariq was taken to more challenging spaces daily, where he began to increase in confidence and learnt to take great care about where he was walking or running. With an improvement in his confidence Tariq quickly began following other children on his visits and was able to be a part of the games they were playing.

Key points

Sometimes the neatness of a school environment doesn't show all the problems a child may be facing, and whilst the staff were aware that Tariq was rather clumsy they had no idea of the extent of his problems. It was only a visit to a new area, with the unpredictability of the outdoors, that it was understood how much additional support Tariq would need. Extra sessions were planned and Tariq quickly gained more balance and coordination in all his large movements, improving his confidence and independence in the outdoor classroom.

The outdoor classroom provides opportunities for children to learn and develop new skills which will improve their fine motor skills as well. Children can learn to hold and use new tools safely, they can learn to wrap rope around objects and eventually tie knots. They can develop their pincer grip, using fingers and thumb to collect small items from the woodland floor. These are all the skills that are developed inside on a daily basis but with a kind of spontaneity that cannot be planned for.

A summary of the benefits of learning in the outdoor classroom

When the positive benefits of teaching and learning in the outdoors are all compiled into one chapter, there remains little doubt that this approach to education is both successful and long-lasting. From the historic background of Froebel and Montessori through to the modern-day approach taken at Bridgwater College in the late twentieth century there seems to be a wealth of evidence to argue a case for more of this style of learning in all settings. I consider that the rapid growth and development of Forest School-inspired learning across the UK supports this theory.

Working in the outdoors has been shown to improve self-esteem, develop confidence and inspire independence, but these are surely qualities that can also be developed through indoor play. Can't behaviour successfully be improved through normal classroom provision, with good management and successful strategies? So why is the outdoors so successful?

Perhaps in this modern world, as in times past, children quite simply thrive on adventure and excitement. Television, computerized games and modern gadgets may provide some thrills, but there is nothing that compares to the feeling of freedom provided by the world outside the classroom. It is unlikely that television programmes will ever replicate the feeling you get when you climb your first tree or roll down a grassy slope. Only catching a living wood louse will show a child how small it is, how intricate its features are and how quickly it can run!

There is still a lot of research to be done on the benefits that can be provided through Forest School and similar opportunities. Now that the first children to access Forest School with Bridgwater College in the early 1990s are entering their twenties, perhaps it is time a detailed study was carried out to consider the long term effects on their lifestyle.

2 The implications for settings using the outdoor classroom

Introduction

This chapter will look at some of the reasons why setting up and working in an outdoor classroom can be such a minefield for the uninitiated. I try to look at the reasons that may be used as an excuse for not implementing outdoor learning and a Forest School approach and then I give a possible solution to the problem. It is important to remind ourselves that each setting is unique and as such will have its own set of difficulties to overcome, but it should also be remembered, during this formative stage of development, that the outcome is always worth it. This is, after all, about setting up a sustainable provision that will benefit the children, and become a highly valued resource in the school community, now and in the future. Taking a positive attitude to these initial inconveniences will be infectious and other problems are likely to be dealt with more efficiently and creatively in the following months. There really are very few problems that cannot be managed by a team of hard working and dedicated staff.

Creating space for an outdoor classroom

For the purpose of setting up an outdoor classroom, running it and visiting it regularly, schools with extensive grounds, wildlife areas and green fields are the most straightforward environments. In such places setting up a creative space for use as a Forest School-style area is relatively simple, in terms of finding the required outside space. For those schools with tarmac playgrounds, small manicured sports fields, perhaps surrounded by housing and industry, creating a wild and safe outdoor classroom is more of a challenge. But not an unachievable one.

The ideal outdoor classroom needs just a few features deemed to be essential for successful opportunities. It requires space, safe within strict boundaries and removed from public admittance. It would be helpful if there was a way of encouraging wildlife to the area, so the children can become more knowledgeable about the plants and animals around them and the changing seasons throughout the school year. It should, of course, be special, perhaps a place which is out of bounds at playtime, not used by local children at weekends and valued by the whole school community for its individuality.

In an ideal world, every school would have a large wooded area, tucked away at the end of a secluded school site. There would be a variety of trees, wild flowers and bushes, a hedge complete with nesting birds and maybe a pond with plant and wildlife. There would be a space for storage, a log circle and a fire pit, some shelter to ensure all-weather use and resources to carry out all manner of exciting and challenging activities. But we all know that schools and teachers are forever being asked to manage on less money, and decreasing budgets ensure that resources are never as complete as we would like and that more school grounds are sold off each year than are bought. So the likelihood of every school being able to achieve the ideal outdoor classroom is very slim. But this should not stand in the way of development and progress in this area of learning.

On a more positive note, most schools in the UK have outside areas of some description, whether the setting is rural or urban. Clearly the amount and type of space varies immensely and the importance placed on that area will depend on the emphasis given to it by the governors, teachers and children. But the way the space is used is changeable; just because it has always been a flat green field doesn't mean it always has to be. The second playground hidden away and neglected makes an ideal place to begin to create a wilder space.

The nature of schools in the modern age means that they are safe, have clear boundaries and are away from public places, and although not especially picturesque, tall security fencing does at least serve the purpose of maintaining a safe environment around the school. In the past, schools have fenced off patches of ground that have been deemed unsuitable for children's play; it is these spaces that now need to be examined and considered in the light of the new idea of outdoor play and the benefits of hands-on exploration. Changing the way these run-down spaces are used doesn't need to cost excessive amounts of money; it needs creative thinking and vision that is workable for that setting. It is pointless to hanker after the ideal Forest School area if your grounds are limited. Such an approach is likely to be the reason why the project does not succeed, so rather than being too idealistic, be realistic. What will work for you, your setting, your staff and most importantly your children?

The next perceived obstacle is wildlife, or maybe the lack of it! Although not essential, is a helpful component for an outdoor classroom; it enhances opportunities for learning and provides an ever-changing environment for finding out, discovering and learning. However it can be created quickly and easily with a few simple flower beds, a vegetable plot, some bird feeders, a pile of rotting logs and, once again, a creative imagination. Such a simple man-made wildlife area can provide opportunities to explore habitat, weather, planting and growing and the impact of man on where we live.

Many of the traditional outdoor activities include creating feeding stations and appropriate habitats for local birds and creatures. Making simple bird feeders will bring some garden birds to visit, a ladybird home over a bed of nettles will encourage these summer visitors to stay, while children watch and learn. Making a compost heap will teach the children about worms and their habits, a paving slab resting across two stones may provide a safe haven for a hibernating hedgehog. Such straightforward activities can become part of the children's learning, and why shouldn't they be instrumental in helping to set up their new outdoor classroom? Children will certainly be more respectful of their space if they have been allowed to take an active part in creating it. Bear in mind though, that if the space has nowhere for children to climb, where will they practise? If the path is gravel, how will they squelch through mud, and if all the prickly brambles and stinging nettles are removed where will the children look for ladybirds or pick blackberries to make pies? If there is no fire pit, how can the children cook potatoes and toast bread, learn to respect the flames and understand how to extinguish it safely?

By simply making the area into a unique space in the school grounds, it has already become a special place; involving the children in its planning, taking their suggestions and allowing them to help with some of the physical aspects, has gone some way towards ensuring they take ownership and maintain some interest. The area should be treated differently to other areas in the school, so asking other teachers to encourage their classes to abide by some simple outdoor classroom rules when they use the area sets it aside from the rest of the school. Many schools prefer their outdoor classroom to be kept as a space used just for that specific time, rather than at playtimes and during lunch breaks.

Some schools have made successful partnerships with local churches and use wild areas of churchyards. These spaces create a unique area, but have problems associated with shared public spaces and storage for resources. The area can never be a permanent space where children take ownership and responsibility; setting up bug traps, making dens and lighting fires can be problematic in such circumstances. Changes in parish councils may even put a stop to the agreement in the long term. However any attempt at using the outdoors as a learning tool can only be beneficial to the children, and should be seen as positive and a step in the right direction.

Other schools have agreements with local Forest School providers, allowing children regular supervised access to more suitable spaces. But in most instances this arrangement involves a short journey either by road or on foot, adding to the pressure of time and school routines. Unfortunately such visits off the main school site involve their own set of rules and requirements, such as parental permission, road safety and additional costs for transport. They also limit the way the outdoor classroom can be used and managed, making impromptu visits, or quick observational opportunities. These are naturally restricted by the distance involved. Once again, though, it is important to view these opportunities as a positive step forward and the concepts, ideas and progress made on these occasions can be revisited back at the school and developed in other ways once back on the main school site.

Health and safety

As with any activity involving children, health and safety is paramount, so what are some of the issues that will affect the development and use of the outdoor classroom? Whilst the subject of risk is discussed elsewhere in this book, it is important to differentiate between the children taking safe risks and the need for a strict health and safety policy. An outdoor classroom environment thrives on the children taking controlled risks, where they learn new skills, make connections and learn from their own successes and mistakes. But an outdoor classroom still needs to be carefully planned and monitored to remain safe at all times. It is essential that adults working in the area know the implications of the activity, can control and modify the session according to the age and ability of the children. They should be experienced in communicating with children and able to clearly share their reasoning with the children.

Managing risk

Involving children in managing risks will be nothing new to them and the children are likely to have taken part in an indoor session where the classroom and playground rules were discussed and written. They will know why those rules need to be there and understand their own role in maintaining them; therefore applying new rules to a new environment should be quite simple. Creating a set of rules to maintain safety is important, but ensuring those rules are repeated regularly with the children is paramount if we are to expect them to remember and use them during their visits. Many establishments spend several minutes on each visit just discussing and recapping the rules and the reasons for needing them. If this is done before the children arrive in the designated area the likelihood of accidents and issues is reduced. Ensuring a child feels safe is essential to their learning, worrying about what might happen will certainly hinder the child's experiences and limit their learning potential. You will almost certainly find a child in your group who, for example, climbs trees every weekend, but if you don't want them climbing trees in the outdoor classroom they will need to know why. Be prepared to answer with logical and reasonable answers in order to ensure this child knows the difference between play at home and learning at school. If you are comfortable about tree climbing, then ensure the rules are clear about expectations and maintaining safety. This is just one example of the type of activity that may take place, others will certainly affect individual sites and people and rules will need to be ever-changing and flexible enough to accommodate the unexpected. It is helpful, though, if the rules for one group of children in the setting are similar to those agreed by each of the other groups using the same space. For example a child being told not to climb by one adult will be confused on a different visit if that leader is allowing this activity to take place. Children respond well to consistency and are more likely to remember and use the rules if they are familiar to them.

Risk-assessing the area will need to be done by the establishment, but will be of more use and relevance if it includes the input of the staff who will be using the area. However good the staff in the school office are, if they never have an opportunity to take children to the outdoor classroom, they are unlikely to know all the pitfalls and problems associated with it. The risk assessment needs to be usable and flexible. New activities will bring new risk and should, if thought necessary, be included.

Risk assessments for outdoor classrooms are likely to include child-to-adult ratios. Whilst there are statutory guidelines for specific age groups that must be adhered to, the school may want its own agreement. Of course, if the outdoor classroom is on site there will be one rule that will be agreed for on-site visits, whilst visits off the premises are likely to attract new requirements. Risk assessment should include adverse weather arrangements. Consider whether your site is safe on a very windy day, would you be concerned for the children's safety if the ditches filled with water? Maybe these opportunities will add a new dimension to the learning taking place, but make sure that you follow any guidelines your school has put in place for your safety and that of the children. Don't use these unexpected events as a reason not to visit, be positive and look for the new learning that will take place and use such occasions as exciting opportunities for impromptu discussion and exploration.

You will need a first-aid kit and preferably a qualified first-aider with you. If you are leaving the premises for your visits to the outdoor classroom it would be essential to ensure that one or more members of accompanying staff were trained in first aid. If you are staying on the school site, it is entirely feasible that the designated first-aider could be called if required. But carrying a simple first-aid kit for minor cuts and grazes, children's medication and a mobile phone for emergency use is the minimum requirement for most settings.

If you decide that you need more adults to support your learning in the outdoors, you may choose to ask parents for their help, but ensuring they have been cleared to work with children is necessary. It should also be a consideration whether their child would be hindered by their presence on every visit, or whether the child's behaviour would be more challenging with a parent and a teacher to work with. Consider a rota of parents to share the time each one has to give, or ask for parents of children in other classes to help you. Some schools have set up opportunities for responsible adults from the local community to work with children as learning partners for reading or writing, why not for exploring and discovering outdoors?

It is likely that some specific activities will need their own risk assessment. Agreeing how to handle tools and light fires safely is essential for all staff and children involved. Using a school pond will have its own set of rules and, as with all other activities, sharing and discussing the rules with the children is more likely to ensure they maintain them. I have not written a list of rules for you to use with each activity because the value of sharing ideas outweighs my expectations, and each setting and group of adults will have different needs. As experienced practitioners we are able to see potential problems and know how to prevent them from becoming unwanted accidents in the future. This attitude should be the foundation of all rule making.

Of course it remains important that the children enjoy their time in the outdoor classroom, so a balance must be found including them in the serious act of rule making, whilst maintaining a sense of enjoyment and excitement. For most children keeping to the rules will be a simple extension to what they already do and should not create any more anxiety than is necessary, but for others it may frighten them and prevent them from feeling comfortable. A well-trained and astute member of staff should be able to reassure them, helping them to relax and enjoy their time.

The role of the supporting adult

There is a great deal resting on the shoulders of the responsible adult accompanying children into the outdoor classroom, so for continuity it is essential that this leader has well-informed and supportive members of staff in their team. Over recent years, with the growing understanding that children need to learn in the outdoors as well as in the indoor environment came a realization that many people working in the childcare and teaching professions were ill-prepared to provide such experiences. As a result many examination boards have adjusted their syllabus to include a module about outdoor learning or Forest School. Level 1, 2 and 3 courses in childcare and education have introduced more importance on the development of children in the outdoors, and many of them include practical work experience in local Forest Schools. The newly accredited Level 3 diploma, Children and Young People's Workforce, includes modules that teach about children's welfare, health and development amongst other units. Within these it would be perfectly feasible that lecturers encouraged their students to consider the importance of learning outside. Bridgwater College, in Somerset, is a good example of how training can be included in childcare qualifications. When Forest School was first introduced to their Early Years Centre, it was considered necessary that the staff expected to run these sessions would need training and encouragement in order to make them successful. It was with this in mind that the college, responsible for introducing Forest School to the UK, created the Level 2 and 3 Forest School awards, which were accredited by the Business and Technology Education Council (BTEC) and subsequently introduced into the college curriculum. From this, the college went on to devise modules for all its courses in the early years, encouraging all students to make Forest School one of their work placements, and shorter courses were run to introduce more people to some of the key skills required to work successfully in the outdoors. With their own success behind them, the college then began to teach the Level 3 qualification as an outreach programme, and other counties and areas across the UK became involved in setting up and managing their own Forest Schools and training programmes. It is now possible to study and experience Forest School in many colleges and higher education institutes across the country, with a choice of exam board and level of qualification.

With the introduction of these courses, early years practitioners have felt empowered to provide more exciting experiences in their places of work. But the introduction of Forest School experiences into schools has been slower; although in recent years it has started to become more widespread, schools still lag behind developments in early years settings. Some of this reluctance can be accounted for because of strict timetabling and compulsory curriculum requirements. Allowing time for exploration and outdoor play takes time away from what has always been considered the more important elements of schooling, such as numeracy and literacy. But often the stumbling block is the reluctance of staff to give priority to outdoor play, and although being outdoors in all weathers is certainly not for all of us, it is rare that you find a child who does not come to love the opportunity outdoor learning provides. It is important that all adults with involvement in outdoor play are positive and cheerful; children are very quick to pick up negativity in adults and this will often spread to the less hardy child. Of course we cannot make adults have a good time while they are outside, but ensuring they have some understanding about the benefits of learning outdoors will hopefully inspire even the most reluctant teacher or assistant.

It is often assumed that in order to run successful outdoor learning experiences adults must have some qualification that states that they are competent; however, adults have been playing with children outdoors for centuries without a piece of paper telling them they are allowed to. A qualification will inspire and help develop confidence in adults, but it is by no means essential. Many practitioners have successfully developed outdoor learning without a certificate that tells them they can. It should be remembered that in many cases an outdoor classroom is just a continuation of a good primary curriculum.

Schools are now beginning to consider ways of developing their outdoor learning, often encouraging one member of staff to become trained to an appropriate level and sharing their experience with others in their setting. This is a successful compromise and whilst ensuring there is one lead teacher, it also helps others to become more involved and therefore more likely to continue with good practice in the future. As Forest School has spread nationwide, small cluster groups have been set up in several areas. These groups provide support to their local institutions, schools and pre-schools and often have the means to provide training at a range of levels. They have become a good source of information, resources and encouragement for those starting out.

Fitting outdoor learning into a crowded timetable

Once the problems associated with space and staffing have been overcome, there is still the issue of when to use the outdoor classroom. As children leave the relative freedom of play and creativity behind them and move into the National Curriculum it becomes harder to find a time when using the outdoor classroom is appropriate. This is where well-trained and inspirational teachers need to look at how they can take elements of the learning outside, whilst still teaching to the required standards. Until recently the art of teaching in the outdoors has not been given enough priority in teacher training courses and the requirement of making it fit to a specific and inflexible curriculum is not one that comes naturally to many people. Even an overwhelming enthusiasm for nature and environment does not qualify an adult to empower young people in the life skills and development that can be acquired through Forest School practices.

Challenging teachers to fit history, literacy and other subjects into an outdoor area is not always the answer. For some children the process of being outside and exploring freely is more valuable than any subject matter will ever be. Children inspired in the outdoors are likely to gain skills that can be transferred back in to the classroom and will be put to good use in other areas of their education. It takes a brave and creative teacher to find the links between true Forest School and the primary curriculum.

Perhaps a way forward would be for the teachers to look at how Forest School is applied in the early years phase. A focus may be given for the time outside, but it is not strictly enforced all exploration is welcomed and celebrated and children are free to follow their own interests.

For example, a small group of children have been asked to consider how the second little pig may have built his house from sticks. What tools would he have needed, how did the rain stay out, how could it have been made stronger? Some of the children have set about collecting sticks and are propping them against a tree, another group is roaming the outdoor classroom looking for a good place to build their shelter. The third group has decided that the second little pig wanted to help the third pig make a house of bricks. They are looking for bricks. Having discovered there are no bricks, they are now building their house using pretend bricks – sticks! Does it matter?

The children are learning about negotiation, listening, idea sharing and working together. This kind of collaborative play, cooperation and excitement is surely relevant in any age group. Had this been a Year 1 literacy lesson that was beginning a topic of fairy tales, all children would have had an exciting, stimulating and memorable experience. This would have helped them to make the required progress when they returned to the classroom, to retell or plan their own story. This may have been a lesson in a Year 6 classroom about the use of creative language in story writing. First-hand experiences such as these would inspire and encourage these children to be more creative in their responses and written work. It may just as easily lead into a science topic about weather, keeping dry, staying warm and selecting the right building materials for the purpose. Within such a simple activity as building stick shelters there are endless opportunities for links to the curriculum for any age group.

Assessment opportunities

Even with the successful planning and delivery of outdoor learning there is still the issue of assessment, and one of the hardest things that some educators and teachers find they have to overcome with this child-led approach is this process of assessment and record keeping. Once again examples can be taken from the early years approach, using cameras, video recordings, making brief observations and simple post-it notes can be applied to any objective. How the teacher uses these jottings and pictures will be different for each individual, but they certainly build a good all-round picture of the child and their development. If a teacher needed more reassurance, more emphasis can be placed on one aspect of the session, such as the use of creative language. Asking a Year 6 child to retell and record their story adding the necessary adjectives will provide the evidence needed and remind the children when they return to the classroom and are expected to recall their work and use it in a different way.

Resourcing your outdoor classroom

There are two trains of thought about setting up an outdoor classroom and resourcing the space. There are the practitioners who believe firmly in the original Forest School concept. They maintain that to be successful you must have a high staff ratio, small groups of children, a special dedicated piece of woodland, the use of tools, everyone in waterproof overalls or trousers, etc. This group of people believe that there has to be a qualified Forest School Leader, because without one, learning can't take place safely.

Then there are those who believe an outdoor classroom is a more modified version of Forest School, where the ethos and principles remain the same, but the approach is less structured and variable. The space can be anywhere, as long as it is seen as special, treated differently to other spaces; it may or may not have trees. The children and staff may be wearing waterproof clothing, but they may just have plenty of warm clothes and dry shoes to change back into afterwards. It is quite likely that the children will use tools and try out new skills, but is not essential. They may just be a small group of children with several well-qualified and confident adults or it may be a whole class with teachers, parents and assistants, learning and developing together as they explore their surroundings. This group is confident that learning will take place with or without a qualified leader.

The first model is the ideal way to run and manage an outdoor classroom, but so often the implications for creating this style of education are so overbearing that outdoor learning becomes a chore and creates its own set of problems, so much so that it might not even get started. The issues with funding to resource the area and clothe the children become an obstacle, or in some cases an excuse for not continuing. Training staff is expensive and requires people to be away from school, creating its own set of problems in the short term. There is no reason why this style of outdoor learning cannot be successful and if this is what you aspire to then you are certainly to be admired for your hard work and dedication. Many nurseries with a higher staff ratio can sustain such an approach; for many schools it is almost certainly an unachievable dream.

The second example is much less dependent on money or highly qualified staff. Enthusiasm and creativity are more important and the children will gain from their experiences and from the opportunity to create their own play and adventure. This model will ensure that outdoor play takes place regardless of budget cuts and red tape. Eventually this model will develop, resources may well be found over the years and staff are likely to become trained, confident and able to lead their children to a deeper understanding and enjoyment of their surroundings. In the meantime, everyone is having fun!

At Sedgemoor Manor Infants, in Bridgwater, the leader happily tells me that she started with no budget, and collected resources by using broken and unwanted items from the classrooms. For example the wooden beads from a broken abacus are now treasure, hidden, waiting to be found by inquisitive children crawling through the long grass. In another school, old metal dustbin lids hang from the trees, waiting to be turned in to musical instruments, rock bands have been formed and orchestras united! An old door frame leads to a world of storytelling where each child goes on their own journey, leading to some of the most creative and inspired writing you would ever expect to see from children under the age of eight years old.

Of course in an age of health and safety and accountability there are some major factors that will need to be considered whichever approach you favour. The site will need to be secure and reasonable fencing will need to determine boundaries and limits for the children's safety. A fire pit will need to be safe, the children sitting an appropriate distance away with water and a fire blanket to hand at all times. The trees must be safe, regularly coppiced and monitored for unsafe branches and observed for those trees that may be dying and are at risk of falling. Any pond or areas of water will need to be behind a locked gate and fence unless the children approach with an adult. Any tools that are used must be locked away and carried in a strong bag, with saw blade covered and with penknives closed. The children will need to be appropriately dressed, which for much of the year will involve wellies and warm coats. Some settings may need to supply spares for those children who don't or are unable to bring their own from home.

So whilst it is relatively easy to entertain the children in the outdoors, ensuring their safety is less straightforward and almost certainly comes with a price attached. It would be very disappointing though, in this age of encouraging more active play, if settings and schools did not place enough importance on this style of learning, and new opportunities for developing outdoor classrooms fell by the wayside due to a lack of funding.

Whether an outdoor classroom can be established and used regularly without large amounts of money will ultimately be down to the people involved. Some schools have very successful outdoor areas in corners of their existing playgrounds, or school fields, where no additional money was required to ensure the children's safety. But it is the creativity of the staff that makes the area special and exciting, and the way in which the space is talked about and used makes it unique and interesting.

The wonderful thing about learning in the outdoors is that many of the resources are natural, already in place and constantly changing and renewing themselves. Watching the leaves change on a tree throughout the year requires nothing, except perhaps a magnifying glass to watch more closely as the new green buds open in the spring, or the autumn leaves change colour. A few cheap tarpaulins make great shelters and a bundle of sisal will help tie them to trees to make dens. Many of the resources already in schools are entirely suitable to be taken outside; bug catchers, mirrors, identification books and charts for mini beasts and plants are just a few examples. Remembering that children have an imagination is crucial; when you were younger and building a den at the end of the garden, I am sure you were very happy to make a carpet of leaves, or a seat using a pile of old sticks. Children in the modern age still have those creative minds and will find a way of making, finding or imagining what they need for their play. Expensive resources are great, but definitely not essential!

Parental support

Having found ways of creating confident and able staff, developed an outdoor learning space and gathered together a few resources on a shoe-string budget, there is still the issue of convincing parents of the value of this style of learning. There is very little doubt that in the early days of Forest School the concept of taking small children into the woodlands and wilderness was a great concern for some parents. These were places where even some adults would have worried for their own safety, never mind that of their child. The ever-present media, its publications and their reports about abductions and accidents only served to heighten parents' anxieties; and whilst the news reports still paint a bleak picture and children do get harmed by strangers, parents are beginning to understand the purpose of Forest School more. Trust in the carers and teachers is essential if schools and nurseries are to be able to work in the outdoors without always worrying about what the parents would be thinking. Some of the parents' fears about their child getting lost or hurt are allayed by previous visits when all has been well and by other parents who have received nothing but good news from their child's visits.

Involving parents

Within schools where the outdoor classroom has been set up and is running successfully parents have often proved to be more enthusiastic than expected! Several settings include some time in the outdoor classroom for the parents to work with their children before the children then go on to visit with their class. These sessions are an opportunity for families to explore and find out about the way their children will be learning. They can be reassured by the teaching staff that their children are in safe hands and that on future visits every precaution will be taken to ensure that no one comes to any harm. It would be wrong to say there are no accidents. Children do trip over, fall into nettles and occasionally get hit with another child's stick, but parents can be given positive messages and experiences that will help them to be confident with their own children in the future. Children who do have minor accidents are few and far between, and they learn resilience and life skills through the way they handle such events.

It should be remembered that for many children and their families, rural life is unfamiliar and as such has perceived hazards and threats that are outside of that particular family's normal comfort zone. Even in modern times, travel out of the cities and into wild spaces is limited for some families, and of course we have to remember there are also people who feel no affinity with the countryside and see little purpose in exposing their children to nature and its elements. These families are often the hardest to reach, but are likely to be the ones for whom learning outdoors can have the most benefit.

Conclusion

There are without doubt many other reasons why outdoor learning should not be successful, but for every problem that is overcome there is a group of children who have seen something, heard something or experienced something that they have not done before. Teaching is about showing children how to share their world with others; outdoor learning can do that.

Of course not all teachers and staff are keen to be outside in all weathers, crouching in the mud with branches in their hair, whilst they hide from a big bad wolf that lives around the corner! But many are, and enthusiasm is infectious. And whilst it is not practical to expect all adults working with young children to see the benefits of learning outdoors, it is realistic to expect the majority of them to be willing to do what is seen by others to be the best for the children in their care. After all, in childcare and school settings we have to teach and provide experiences that we are less than enthusiastic about, but maintaining a positive outlook is essential for the children and there is little doubt that children will learn from our behaviour and opinion.

For many of us the pleasure gained from watching a young child find a ladybird or crawl into their own shelter outweighs the red tape involved in beginning a programme of outdoor learning.

3 | Using topic-based learning in the outdoor classroom

Introduction

The following series of ideas and plans based on topic work is here to provide some inspiration for teachers and practitioners wanting to get their children outdoors more frequently. With the ethos of the outdoor classroom supporting cross-curricular activities I show how it can be used as an opportunity to learn across several areas of the relevant curriculum. Where I make links to the curriculum, the list is by no means comprehensive; you will certainly find other aspects of specific subjects that work within this framework. Of course, each topic is just suggestions and ideas; how you develop the plans will depend upon your children, how many adults you have and what your outdoor classroom area has to offer. But I hope that these ideas will help new and experienced outdoor classroom users find the links with both the Early Years Foundation Stage (EYFS) and the National Curriculum for Key Stage 1, and go on to run successful sessions in the outdoors.

The topics are divided into three sections. The first shows how children can be introduced to some simple Forest School style-activities, through the regular use of the outdoor classroom. Whilst it is not necessary that the lessons be taught in any particular order, they are planned to follow each other if that is required. The next set of activities relates to the curriculum area of Literacy, in particular traditional tales and using the outdoors to inspire and develop children's imagination. These lessons are arranged to be progressive, but as with all teaching there is scope to add additional learning and develop the plans according to your particular cohort. The final set of lesson ideas focuses on numeracy and there are ideas that work towards the strands of numbers and counting, measurement, size and shapes, pattern and colour. These can be taught in the order that works for your classroom planning.

For each activity, I have included ideas for adults in their role of supporter and also some more directed suggestions if you want to steer the children towards a particular outcome. Each topic has a resource list and health and safety reminders. You will find it useful to add your own specific requirements to make it appropriate for your setting.

Through my own experiences the subjects of literacy and numeracy are the ones so often quoted as being difficult to accommodate in the outdoor classroom. It is relatively easy to take scientific learning outside, to create inspirational art and design lessons within the natural world and to see how physical skills can be challenged and developed

Photo 3.1 Staying safe in the outdoor classroom

Health and safety

As with every visit to the outdoor classroom, ensure children are familiar with the rules they have made in order to keep them safe. Reiterate why we have these rules.

Fire safety

Your setting will have its own rules about fires; remind the children what they are. They should include: how to move safely around the fire area, what is a safe distance to sit from the fire, how the children should approach a fire with an adult, how the children should behave in the fire pit area with and without a fire. Children should be repeatedly reminded about these rules and any serious breaches need to be dealt with appropriately. Please don't frighten the children, rather make sure you teach them to respect the fire and behave accordingly.

Stick carrying

Remind children that they can only carry sticks as long as their arms, but if they need longer ones they can ask for some help. Demonstrate how the children can carry a long stick with a friend, or by pulling it behind them.

Staying in a safe place

What are your rules for keeping the children in the outdoor classroom area? Are they allowed to climb fences and gates? Do they know they should stay in the area, unless they leave with a member of staff? Each setting will need to have clear and consistent guidelines for this aspect of working outdoors.

in such a diverse environment. Sometimes a starting point makes a difference to how you approach teaching outside. This chapter is to help you understand how simple it can be to take your class outside and provide a new learning experience.

Please remember though, that some of the best learning in the outdoor classroom is spontaneous and as such cannot be planned for. In my experience once the children have been introduced to some ideas about how they can use the space and the kinds of games and activities they can do there, they will develop their own way of learning that will, ultimately, ensure they meet some of the objectives during the series of lessons.

Introduction to Forest School skills

This series of lessons has been created to give a taste of some of the activities that have become closely linked with Forest School over the years since its inception. The idea is to give children time to explore their environment and to know how they can use the area as a way to enhance their own learning. It will give children the confidence they need for successful learning in the future and the courage they need to apply their own ideas and enthusiasm to new activities.

Whilst these activities do not have a specific subject focus they are clearly linked across the whole curriculum, giving children a breadth of education that is not always possible in a classroom. As with all activities in the outdoor classroom there needs to be an emphasis on praise and encouragement with importance placed on even the smallest achievement.

These activities can be progressive, although each one can also be used as a separate experience or linked in to other lessons that may take place alongside them.

Prior learning/experience

There is no expectation that the children will have had much experience of using the outdoors, but it is always helpful if the area is familiar and that the children have had a chance to explore in previous sessions. These simple activities are an opportunity for them to find out about this environment and to learn about how they can stay safe and enjoy these diverse opportunities.

Remember children using the outdoor classroom for the first time will need to be given a set of rules to help keep them safe and to enable them to explore without inhibitions and concerns for their safety.

Fitting Forest School experiences into the Early Years Foundation Stage

This topic works towards the following aspects of the curriculum being used in either a nursery or reception class and in Key Stage 1 classes.

Personal, social and emotional development

Children will have opportunities to try new ideas, share experiences and discuss them in small, familiar groups. They will begin to show an awareness of the needs of those children they are working with, showing respect for others' views and suggestions.

Through these activities children will begin to learn that they can expect others to treat them, their ideas and views with respect and understanding. They will have opportunities to develop relationships with both adults and children, taking turns, sharing, and understanding the need for some rules to maintain safety and good behaviour.

Communicating, language and early literacy

Children will have opportunities to interact with others, negotiating plans and activities and taking turns in conversation. They will respond to what they hear and see with relevant comments and responses. Children will be able to expand their vocabulary, exploring the meanings of new words through first-hand exploration. They will begin to speak clearly and with confidence, showing an awareness of the listener. The children have opportunities to use talk to organize, sequence and clarify their thinking, feelings, ideas and events.

Mathematics

Children will use mathematical language to compare quantities and lengths, greater, smaller, longer and shorter. They will use everyday words to describe position, shape and size. They will have opportunities to solve mathematical problems using developing ideas and methods.

Finding out about our world

Children will investigate objects and materials using all of their senses as appropriate. They will find out about and identify some of the features of living things, objects and events they observe. Through these activities children can look at similarities, differences, patterns and change, asking questions about why things happen. The children have the opportunity to build and construct with a range of materials, selecting the tools and techniques they need to be successful.

Children will observe, find out about and identify features in the place they live and in the natural world. They will explore their environment, and be able to discuss their likes and dislikes about their findings.

Physical development

Children will learn to move through uneven territory with control and coordination, travelling over and under obstacles, balancing and climbing. They will develop a sense of awareness of their space and others around them. They will be finding out about the changes that happen to their body when they are active. Children will use tools and equipment, small and large, with increasing control. They will develop the necessary skills to keep themselves and others safe.

Creativity and imaginative play

Children will learn to respond to what they see, hear, touch and smell. They will be able to express their thoughts and ideas in an increasing number of ways by using tools, materials, and imaginative role play. Children will have ample opportunity to explore colour, texture, shape, space and form in two and three dimensions.

Working with the National Curriculum at Key Stage 1

Literacy

Children will learn to speak clearly, choosing appropriate words and with some organization of content. They will learn the conventions of conversation, taking turns in speaking, listening to others and taking their viewpoints into consideration. They will be learning to give reasons for their opinions and actions. Through effective listening the children will learn to sustain concentration, make relevant comments and ask questions to clarify their understanding.

Numeracy

Children will learn to select and use appropriate mathematical ideas to solve problems involving space, shape and measures. They will develop an understanding of the vocabulary involved in some simple mathematical concepts, learn to explain and communicate their ideas effectively.

Science

Children will use first-hand experiences to find out for themselves, thinking about what might happen before deciding what to do. They will have opportunities to ask questions and work out how they can find the answers to them.

Children will learn to follow instructions to keep themselves and others safe from harm. They will explore using all of their senses as appropriate, communicating what happens to others. They will be able to make simple comparisons, reviewing their work and explaining what happened to others.

Children will learn aspects of life processes, green plants, classification, and will discover about their own environment and the things which live within it.

Foundation subjects (geography, history, art and design technology, physical education, PSHE and citizenship)

Children will learn to select the appropriate tools and materials for the task, planning their next steps, through evaluation and comparison.

Children will learn to identify and describe features of places and locations, comparing landscapes and places using developing vocabulary.

Activity 1: Forest School skills – lighting a fire

This activity will help the children to realise that there are elements of learning outside that carry some risk and which need their own particular set of rules. The children will learn about respecting their outdoor classroom and develop some responsibility for their own behaviour in a new environment.

Teaching opportunity

Allow the children to explore the outdoor classroom freely, remembering the rules, looking for changes and returning to previous activities. Back in the log circle or meeting place ask the children to share their findings and discuss what they have seen or found out. This can become a part of each visit to the area and helps children to become aware of the world around them.

The main activity today will be about fire lighting, so recapping the rules about fire safety is of paramount importance.

The children will need to collect a range of sticks in order to help light the fire. Discuss the need for small, dry sticks for the first stage, building up to bigger sticks once the fire is well alight. Ask each child to collect sticks they think are suitable for the first stage. Demonstrate to the children how they can use the sticks to build a fire structure before lighting it.

Children can have a go at building their own fire structure, without actually lighting it.

Light the fire laid in the fire pit and ask the children to collect the next size sticks and begin to bundle them ready to dry.

Discuss how the fire can be made safe.

Safely put out the fire.

Key Stage 1 extension activity

Discuss the three elements required for fire lighting – air, fuel and heat and how each is represented.

Explain that if we remove one of the elements the fire will go out. Talk about how we can take away an element and what will happen.

Key questions

What kind of wood do we need to light a fire? Should it be wet or dry? Why?

If we put sand/water on the fire, what would happen? Why?

Adults

It is important that all adults know and adhere to the same set of rules about fire safety during this session. One adult must always be alongside the fire.

Children will be able to collect and lay their own fires, so adults will be best utilized by asking questions, generating conversation and supporting learning through discussions in small groups.

Children approaching the fire will need an adult close by at all times.

Success criteria

Children will have found out about fire lighting. They will be able to identify suitable wood and know how to lay the sticks in order to light a fire. They will have worked with others to discuss the merits of the sticks they are collecting and will have helped others to lay sticks ready for a fire.

Some children will be able to discuss the elements required for a fire to light successfully and how to extinguish it before leaving the area.

All children will have a good understanding of why we need rules for fire safety.

Activity 2: Forest School skills – cooking over a fire

This lesson, although it could be used on its own, follows on from Lighting a Fire. The children can begin to see that their hard work has a purpose, that they need to collect and dry firewood if they want to cook in the future. There is also the introduction of tools in this lesson, so careful consideration should be given to adult ratios.

Teaching opporunities

Today the children will be learning to cook using the fire so they should be familiar with fire safety rules before you carry out these activities.

Show the children a leaf from a hazel or elder tree and ask them to try and find a tree that has these leaves. Cut some long branches from these trees, about one metre long and show the children how to carefully strip the leaves from them, to leave a long straight branch.

Using a potato peeler demonstrate to the children how they can strip the soft bark from their stick. The peeler should always be scraped away from the child and the child will need close supervision. They can use these sticks for cooking.

Light a fire and recap the fire safety rules and the elements needed for a successful fire (see previous activity).

Give the children a choice of food to cook on the fire – marshmallows, crumpets, bread and teacakes. What do the children think will happen to each one when it is cooked? Discuss.

Working with one or two children to each adult, approach the fire safely with the selected food on the end of the child's hazel stick. Explain that the food should be cooked in the embers of the fire, rather than the flame. Discuss the changes that take place.

Key Stage 1 extension activity

If the children are familiar with using potato peelers they can be introduced to using a pen knife. The same strict rules apply about scraping away from the body and whilst sitting down. Children should be taught to close the pen knife or to stick the open knife into the ground beside them to maintain safety.

Key questions

What will happen to the marshmallow/bread etc? Why do you think that? Were you right? Can you explain what happened?

Adults

Fire safety must be maintained at all times and the same rules should be followed by each adult. Support the children in remembering and applying the rules when they are in close proximity to the fire.

A similar approach should be taken when children are using pen knives or potato peelers and safety rules should be strictly enforced throughout the activity. Careful questioning will help the children to consider what they can see and support their improving vocabulary.

Success criteria

Children will have had an opportunity to cook over the fire. They will have chosen their food, predicted what will happen, watched the changes and made observations. They will have eaten the food and compared their prediction with the actual outcome.

All children will have tried to identify a specific tree suitable for the purpose and will have used a peeler or small pen knife to peel away the bark. They will have a good understanding of the need for safety rules during their time in the outdoor classroom.

Photo 3.2 Making a woven panel of sticks and branches

Activity 3: Forest School skills – making a windbreak

This activity allows children opportunities to work closely in a group. They will learn to discuss and make decisions with others, accepting others' ideas as valid and important. They can share prior experiences and model how the task can be carried out successfully. There is the use of tools in this lesson so the ratio of adults should be considered and it will important to reiterate relevant rules.

Teaching opportunities

In this activity the children will be making a panel using natural materials. When completed and added to others this panel can be made into a shelter or a windbreak.

For this activity the children will be introduced to a pruning saw and there will need to be additional safety rules in place to ensure the safety of everyone.

Begin by showing the children the saw and asking them to explain what they see and share their experiences in the past. Point out key elements of a saw: the teeth, the handle, etc. What do the children think it is used for? Discuss what size branches and trees we are most likely to use it on. Why would it be no good if we wanted to fell a tree? Discuss what would we use if we wanted to cut other materials.

If you have access to hazel trees take the children to look for long straight branches that can be cut down. If you do not have trees, show the children some branches that you have cut from elsewhere and gathered yourself.

Demonstrate how to use the saw sensibly to cut some long sticks.

Working in small groups show the children how they can use the saw themselves to cut the wood to similar lengths. You will need eight long sticks (1.5–2 metres).

In an adult-supported small group begin to tie two branches together at right angles. The aim will be to create a large square shape, fixed firmly at each corner and with two horizontal sticks and two vertical sticks within the square, making a panel suitable for weaving.

When completed, ask the children to consider what we can use to weave through the panel to make it more substantial. Take suggestions and with supervision allow the children to select an appropriate tool to cut down the greenery they require. Support them in weaving it into their panel.

Key Stage 1 extension activity

Ask the children to find appropriate trees by identifying them using ID charts. Hazel is the most suitable for this activity. Demonstrate how to fix the rope to a stick using a clove hitch; help the children practise making their own knot.

Key questions

Ask the children to consider how the panel can be made more stable (by adding more sticks to the framework).

What will happen to the material that is woven through, and why?

Is there any way that we can make our panels living?

Adults

Demonstrate fixing rope using appropriate knots and encourage the children to persevere themselves. Support the children in using new tools and ensure safety rules are met. Question the children, encouraging them to think about how we can use natural materials in our everyday lives.

Success criteria

Children will have contributed towards a purposeful object and will have some ideas about the uses of natural materials. They will understand how to use tools safely and will know that some tools are used for specific jobs.

Some children will be able to discuss how their panel can be improved and adapted for other situations and purposes.

Activity 4: Forest School skills – creating a woodland shelter

This activity is aimed at encouraging some of the skills developed through personal, social and emotional schemes of work – cooperation, turn taking, discussion and sharing ideas – whilst providing an opportunity for the children to design their own science experiment.

Teaching opportunities

Give each group of children a large envelope explaining that it is has something very important inside that must not get wet.

The children's task will be to find somewhere dry and safe to keep the envelope. They can use any of the resources from the kit as well as the materials they can find around the outdoor classroom.

Allow the children time to talk, plan and make their safe environment. Introduce the idea that it may rain later that day, that the next day may be windy, etc. Discuss a timescale with the children before they begin. Will the envelope stay hidden for the rest of that day/week, etc?

At an agreed time, children can return to their envelope to find out what has happened to it. Discuss their findings with them and ask the groups to work out a plan that may improve their hiding place and why they think that will work.

As a whole class, share experiences and try to create the perfect hiding place, taking into account all the results.

Take photos for the children to annotate at a future time.

Key Stage 1 extension activity

Encourage the use of appropriate vocabulary to describe their location: dry, damp, waterproof, etc.

This activity can be used as part of a scheme of work about materials and their properties and children should be encouraged to consider their experiment in light of any work already taken place.

Children should be encouraged to organize their group in order to share, take turns and explain their thoughts openly.

Key questions

How have you encouraged each other and ensured you are working fairly together?

Explain why you have chosen your location, why do you think it is the most suitable place?

What will happen to the envelope if it rains? Is there a way you can make the safe place watertight?

Adults

Some children will need to be supported with helpful suggestions to begin their task, they may need an adult to make reference to previous relevant experience. Adults can also help children to organize their group, encouraging them to share the tasks amongst them and listen and respond to each other's ideas.

Success criteria

Each group will have worked well together, sharing ideas and experiences with each other. Some children will have worked out the most appropriate way to ensure the envelope remains dry; others will have had the chance to try ideas and modify their plan. All children will have had an opportunity to share their findings and evaluate their work with others.

An introduction to traditional tales in the outdoor classroom

This topic has been developed to work alongside some of the units in the Key Stage 1 Primary Strategy. But as with all outdoor classroom work it covers many areas of the curriculum, not just the one it sets out to achieve.

Prior learning/experiences

There is an assumption that this topic will form part of a unit of work being carried out in the classroom as well as in the outdoor environment. Children will need to know some of the traditional fairy tales used, in particular The Three Little Pigs, Little Red Riding Hood or Jack and the Beanstalk. The emphasis, as with most tasks outdoors, is on doing and taking part, rather than writing and providing evidence of learning. That aspect of the work will be more easily achieved back in a classroom, when the children are inspired and enthusiastic.

   This topic works towards the following aspects of the curriculum being used in either a nursery or reception class and in Key Stage 1 classes.

Fitting the experiences into the Early Years Foundation Stage

Personal social and emotional development

Children will be interested, excited and motivated to learn. They will become more confident to try new activities, initiate ideas and speak in a familiar group. Children will learn to work harmoniously with adults and children in small and large groups but also to be independent in their choices and selection of resources. They will learn how to behave in the outdoor environment and find out how they and their friends can stay safe.

Communicating, language and early literacy

Children will enjoy listening to and using spoken and written language, and readily turn to it in their play and learning. They will have opportunities to interact with others, make plans and share ideas. Using talk to organize thinking, sequence ideas, imagine and recreate roles and experiences, children will be able to develop listening skills and understand the rules of turn taking in conversation.

Mathematics

Children will select appropriate materials to make their home, making approximate and non standard measurements for roof materials and string. They will have considered the size and space required in order to fit their group, and made adjustments accordingly.

Finding out about our world

Children will be able to investigate objects and materials by using their senses as appropriate and will find out about living things in their environment. They will observe and identify features in the place where they live and in the wider world, recognizing that all places are not the same. They will begin to understand that in different cultures we have different ideas about aspects of living.

Physical development

Children will experience using a range of equipment and materials for construction, they will learn to move safely around the outdoor area, negotiating their way safely through uneven terrain. They will learn to move with confidence, control and coordination, showing an awareness of space.

Creativity and imaginative play

Children will have opportunities to express their learning through role play, retelling stories and through appropriate songs. They will consider how to make their hiding place less visible, using colours that will help camouflage them and their shelter.

Working with the National Curriculum at Key Stage 1

Literacy

Children will explore familiar themes and characters through improvisation and role-play, learning to retell the stories and ordering events using appropriate story language. They will be able to present parts of their story to an audience and will learn to evaluate their performance and that of others. They will learn to share ideas, negotiate with others, ask and answer questions and extend their vocabulary.

Numeracy

Children will be using mathematics in real context, learning to use non-standard measurements and use appropriate language. They will be using positional language, describing placement of objects and giving directions to others.

Science

Children will explore their local environment using their senses; they will be able to find out about similarities and differences. The children will be deciding what materials are fit for the purpose and testing them in context. They will be finding out about habitats and suitable locations for wolves according to their perceived needs.

Information communication and technology

Children will use digital cameras to record their work, learning to download and print pictures on their return to the setting.

Foundation subjects (geography, history, art and design technology, physical education, PSHE and citizenship)

Children will have made observations about the environment, communicated information through symbols on maps and used these simple maps and keys to help locate relevant places in the outdoor classroom. They will have used some geographical language, practised some fieldwork skills and will be able to talk about features of the school grounds.

Photo 3.3 Building a house of sticks

Activity 1: Telling a story in the outdoor classroom

This lesson is designed to give you a general idea of how literacy can be taken outdoors. The choice of traditional tale is just an example, but the story of the Three Little Pigs lends itself very well to a large unit of work in the outdoor classroom.

Teaching opportunities

Select a traditional tale that the children have been working with in the setting, and before the session place some clues to the story around for children to find.

For this example I am using the story of the Three Little Pigs, but it works equally well with other traditional tales.

Send the children to explore the area, can they find any clues to a story? Ask them to consider the story, characters in the story and importance of the clue. Bring children back together to share their finds, what story can it be? Wolf prints, a bale of straw, a pile of sticks, etc. Discuss appropriate stories and decide which to retell together. Use familiar patterns of language and ask the children to help with parts of the story. For example they can huff and puff, speak the parts of the little pigs, etc.

Include detail about the setting, the tall dark trees in the forest and the bright green grass in the field. Make these details particular to your school.

Ask the children to go and find an appropriate place for the pigs to hide from the wolf. Allow the children plenty of time to explore and be challenged. Should they build something, hide behind something, is it big enough? How can it be made bigger?

Key Stage 1 extension activities.

Give the children an outline plan of the outdoor classroom and mark where shelters can be built. Ask the children to use the map to locate an area before building their shelter. Returning to the whole class, ask each group to mark on the map the location of their shelter, using a key. Other groups can use maps to look for shelters and evaluate whether they believe all children use the right places on the maps.

Key questions

Can we all get in? How can we make it better? What would the wolf be thinking when he found their hiding place? Which way would he come in? How can we stop that? Why is your idea better than someone else's? Perhaps it's not – why?

Adults

Support children in their exploration from a distance and allow them to negotiate with their friends, help them to reach a compromise if necessary and encourage discussion about plans and ideas. Praise children for their ideas and achievements however small.

Some children may need some physical support, to tie up shelters, move large logs. Help when necessary but always encouraging the child to try on their own.

Success criteria

Children will have participated in small group and whole class work, they may have contributed, asked or answered questions. They will have used a range of available resources to consider and make a home to hide in. They will be able to discuss their reasoning behind the choices they have made and may be able to discuss how it can be modified.

The children will be able to retell the story using the conventions of storytelling. They will have begun to think about the characters and will be able to share their ideas with others. On returning to the indoor setting they will be enthusiastic to continue play and work on the same theme, recording their learning and developing their play experiences independently.

Key Stage 1 children will be able to demonstrate how to locate places on a simple map using features of the landscape as guides. They will be able to discuss some of the problems associated with using maps.

Activity 2: Retelling a familiar story

Remind children about the traditional tale you have been working on in your previous session. What characters did it have, what did the children build, was it successful?

Teaching opportunities

This week the children will be using the same story, but they will need to add more elements to it and learn to retell the story in the outdoor classroom. Encourage the children to relocate or rebuild their original hiding place and to carry out the activities.

Activities

Introduce the concept that stories can be changed. Many stories weren't written down for hundreds of years and therefore there are lots of different versions of the same story. Consider how the story of the Three Little Pigs ends; do all the children have the same ending?

In small self-chosen groups, ask the children to consider the task and share initial ideas with an adult. Send them to explore and discuss their story, give a set amount of time and some warnings about when time is running out. During their time they should consider how they can change their story ending. Children should be encouraged to retell the story using the new ending; they can use elements of the outdoor classroom to support their storytelling and will have a selection of appropriate resources to use.

Key Stage 1 extension activity

Encourage children to add more detail into their story, using adjectives to enhance their version. They can act out the story, using a range of voices to highlight the different characters and they will be able to tell their story on the go, moving around the outdoor classroom as they retell.

Key questions

What additional language can you add to your story to make it more interesting?
 Can you change the tone of your voice to imply good and bad events in the story?
 How could you let the audience know what your character is like?

Adults

Allow the children to work as a group with as little intervention as possible. As with all outdoor tasks some children may need some support with the physical skills, but should be encouraged to try, and be praised when they have. Recognize good contribution and team work and reward accordingly.

Challenge the children to use the space to tell the story and consider how they can use the environment as a part of the story.

Model using some descriptive language and the change of voice tone to imply the meaning of the words and the characteristics of the characters.

Success criteria

The children will be familiar with a traditional tale and will have had an opportunity to retell their version of the story. The children will be speaking clearly and the audience will have recognized the changes that have been made.

The children will evaluate their own performance and consider how they could improve their work in the future. All children will have been able to critically evaluate other groups' work and will be able to explain what they liked and did not like.

Activity 3: Storytelling from a different culture

This is a lesson that, whilst still based on storytelling, moves towards the oral storytelling from other cultures. Once again it is a plan that can be adapted and suited to fit your other classroom activities.

Teaching opportunitites

Explain that Native American Indians didn't write their traditional stories down on paper, but that the tale was passed on to the next generation through storytelling. Each time the story was told small details could be changed and eventually a story could have changed altogether and be unrecognizable from the original story. To help them retell the story without too many important changes the Native Americans made something called a story stick. They would carve patterns and symbols on to the stick, attach bits and pieces and use these sticks to recall the order of the story.

Show the children a story stick that you have made that will help you tell the story that you have been learning (I am using the Three Little Pigs as an example). Retell the story showing the children how each part of the stick reminds you of something. For example, the three scratches remind you of the three pigs; some straw tied on reminds you that the straw house was the first house and so on.

Activities

The children can make their own story stick using the natural materials they can find around them. With support, they can use tools to make marks on their stick and string to tie the items on. The children should consider carefully what aspects of their story need to be represented and which bits they know they will remember.

Key Stage 1 extension activity

As the children use their stick to retell the story, encourage them to add more detail, without adding more to their stick. For example, they may have attached a bundle of brown leaves to represent the wolf, but they can say 'the big bad wolf stood up and showed his big white teeth and shouted …'

Key questions

What do you want to attach to your stick and what will it represent? How will it remind you of the story?

Is it necessary that all the detail is included? What could you remove without losing the storyline?

Adults

Use plenty of encouragement and praise for all achievements, however small. Some children will need support tying things, but should be encouraged to help. If tying is too tricky, provide children with some sticky tape to wrap around instead.

Help the child to introduce new and exciting words into their story, without losing the storyline. Suggest the children share their progress with each other and help each other with the more physical aspects of creating a story stick.

Children using a pen knife or potato peeler will need adult supervision.

Success criteria

All children will have attempted to make a story stick and some children will have successfully created a whole story. Other children may have just made the title. Children will have located natural materials and learnt to tie them to sticks. They will have considered how to make their storytelling interesting and will have added descriptive language at relevant places. Some children will successfully evaluate their own work and that of other children.

Activity 4: A celebration of storytelling

Children will have already used the outdoor classroom to explore storytelling. They have built places to represent parts of the story, they have changed elements of the story and retold them again in the outdoor classroom with a small audience and they have been introduced to the idea that they can use natural materials to represent elements of their story to help them recall it.

This week will be a celebration of storytelling. The children can use any of the skills they have been finding out about to tell a story. Some children may need a familiar tale to guide them, others will want to create their own story with some of the characters from the stories they have been using.

Teaching opportunities

Allow the children access to all the resources that have been available over the last few weeks and encourage them to make a choice about what story they want to retell or create. Some children will want to work on their own and others in groups, either will be fine. Give the children plenty of time to consider what they are doing and then collect everyone together. Discuss a few examples of work already started and support others with ideas and suggestions, encouraging the child to make the decisions themselves.

Allow further time for more play and learning before asking children if they would like to share their story.

Key Stage 1 extension activities

Children in Key Stage 1 should be able to present their story in their own way. But in order to create new learning opportunities, give the children a map which shows where there are particular storytelling elements – where the wolf lives, the beanstalk, Little Red Riding Hood's, house etc. Ask the children to try and include at least one of these in their storytelling journeys.

Key questions

What is your story about? Is it a story I will know, or are you making a new one? Who is your main character, what are they like? Will I like them? Why?

How will you remember your story? Can you explain what you will be doing to help you?

Adults

Use lots of praise and encouragement and be enthusiastic and excited with the children. Support the children with their decisions about how to retell the story, remind them what they found useful in previous weeks. If the children stray from the task, encourage them back by joining in role play experiences with them. Do not get anxious if the children have moved away from storytelling; observe, listen and record what they are doing in a positive way.

Success criteria

Some children will have created a story they can retell using some of the elements of the previous week's work. Some children will have developed their main character and can explain how their story might work. Children will have explored the environment and found ways to use it to develop their learning. All children will know a familiar tale and will recognize a few characteristics of the people in it.

Photo 3.4 Stories can be improved and developed by adding sound effects to the storytelling

Numeracy outside the classroom

This set of lesson ideas has been written to introduce you to the idea of using the outdoors to extend the learning going on in the classroom. Whilst this series is predominantly based on numeracy, it becomes clear that there are many links to be made with other subject areas, and with some tweaking to make them suitable for your establishment they are ready to be implemented.

Prior learning/experiences

It is helpful if the children are familiar with the outdoor classroom, its rules and the range of environments. The children are likely to recognize some shapes and will be able to apply this to the slightly irregular shapes around them. They will know about colour and pattern and will be able to link this to new learning experiences. Some understanding of measurements would be helpful as would an understanding of the concepts associated with size – big, small, tall and short, etc.

Fitting the experiences into the Early Years Foundation Stage

Personal social and emotional development

Children will be more confident to try new activities, initiate ideas and speak in a familiar group. They will be interested, excited and motivated to learn, working harmoniously with adults and children in small and large groups. They will discover how it feels to be independent in their choices and selection of resources, learning from their mistakes and sharing their successes. They will know how to behave in the outdoor environment and learn how they and their friends can stay safe. The children will learn to take turns and share fairly, recognizing the need for some social rules for good working relationships. They will form good relationships with the adults around them, discovering how they can show their emotions appropriately.

Communicating, language and early literacy

Children will learn how to interact and negotiate with others, making plans and sharing ideas and suggestions. They will be learning to use talk to clarify their thinking, feelings and problem solving. They will learn to use appropriate vocabulary to explain their tasks and to evaluate what they have been doing.

Mathematics

Children will be using non standard measures to explore the concepts of long and short, tall and short, narrow and wide. They will be problem solving in real life contexts, planning and experimenting to develop their mathematical thinking. They will be exploring shape and pattern, symmetry and colour and using mathematical language to make observations and describe what they find out.

Finding out about our world

Children will be exploring pattern, shape, colour and texture in their environment, noticing similarities and differences in their surroundings. They will observe, discuss and monitor their world, noting features that identify the landscape around them. The children will be able to ask questions about why things happen and use their own skills to try to find out the answers.

Physical development

Children will experience using a range of equipment and materials for construction; they will learn to move safely around the outdoor area, negotiating their way safely through uneven terrain. They will learn to move with confidence, control and coordination, showing an awareness of space. Through the manipulation of tools and materials children will improve hand–eye coordination and fine motor skills.

Creativity and imaginative play

Children will explore colour and texture in two and three dimensions, using natural and manmade materials. They will express their ideas and respond to their new experiences in a variety of creative ways using their imagination and previous experiences to create new learning.

Working with the National Curriculum at Key Stage 1

Literacy

Children will have opportunities to use associated mathematical language through structured and independent play. They will share their ideas and suggestions with others, learning to speak clearly and succinctly for all to understand. Children will learn about turn taking in conversations and negotiation in play and learning, exploring how to validate their ideas with appropriate reasons. They will learn to listen to others and make relevant comments, remembering specific points of interest in order to clarify them through questioning.

Numeracy

Children will be using mathematics in real context, learning to use non standard measurements and use appropriate language. They will be using positional language, describing placement of objects and giving directions to others. Children will be able to make estimations, adding and grouping objects. They will identify shapes, discuss the properties of specific shapes and note the differences between them. Children will have opportunities to visualize common 2D shapes and 3D solids and identify shapes from pictures of them in different positions and orientations. They will sort, make and describe shapes, referring to their properties.

Some activities will allow children to explore and estimate, compare and measure lengths using standard and non standard measures.

Science

Children will learn about using their own observations and evidence in order to answer their own questions and solve everyday problems. They will find out about planning their own investigations and using first-hand experience to answer questions. Children will have opportunities to recognize fair testing and will make simple comparisons. They will be able to review what they have done and be given opportunities to share their outcome with others.

Photo 3.5 Looking at shapes in the outdoor classroom: these boys have noticed the shape of the roof on the round house

Information communication and technology

Children will become familiar with digital cameras in order to record their work and outcomes. They will learn about collecting and retrieving information from different sources, and when returning to the classroom will be able to present their work in different ways using a selection of appropriate software and by printing their photos.

Foundation subjects (geography, history, art and design technology, physical education, PSHE and citizenship)

Children will have used a range of physical skills, fine and gross motor. They will have moved with care and consideration to others, improving their balance and coordination. The children will have had opportunities to work with others, negotiate, turn take and share. They will have looked at colour, pattern and texture.

Activity 1: Shapes and the environment

Explain that the session today will have a focus on shapes. What can the children tell you about shapes? Can they describe their properties?

Introduce children to the concept that everything has a shape, some are regular and some are not, show some examples.

Teaching opportunities

Using some sticks, ask the children to make some shapes on the ground and explain what they have done. Encourage the use of shape-related mathematical vocabulary: sides, edges, corners, equal and unequal. Discuss how the children can make the sticks the correct length for their shape. Explain that some of these shapes could be fixed into place by tying them together.

Encourage the children to look around them and find shapes in their environment that they can copy – rectangular tree trunks, triangular roofs and circular flowers. Can they recreate the shapes on the ground and turn them into a picture or tie them together to make a mobile?

Key Stage 1 extension activities

Encourage the children to make several shapes the same and try to fit them together. Can they make shapes that are symmetrical and what might some of the problems be associated with this (for example, irregular sticks)?

If they were going to turn their shape into a three-dimensional shape, how many sides would they need to make? How many sticks will they need?

Key questions

What shape are you making? How many sides/edges will it need? Can you work out how many sticks you will need to use?

If it was to be three-dimensional, do you know what shape it could become? How many sticks would you need for that shape?

Adults

Allow the children to discover their own shapes in the environment and make suggestions about their names and properties. Prompt children to consider some of the key questions. Encourage the children to make accurate comparisons of their sticks, measuring them against each other. Support children with the physical aspects of tying the sticks together, whilst encouraging children to try. Praise any efforts and results.

Support the children if their learning takes them away from the tasks, making mental notes about their play and interactions.

Success criteria

Children will be able to find some shapes in the outdoor classroom and its surrounding areas. They will know the names of some basic two- and three-dimensional shapes and be able to discuss similarities and differences between them. They will have an understanding of the vocabulary associated with the properties of shape and be able to recognize how a two-dimensional shape is associated with a three-dimensional one.

Key Stage 1 children will be able to find a symmetrical shape and replicate it accurately, recognizing the importance of equality on both sides. They will be able to discuss their ideas using appropriate mathematical language.

Activity 2: Measurement and size

This activity will help children to become more independent in their learning, finding their own resources and making their own decisions. They will need to work well with others and apply classroom experiences to the task.

Teaching opportunities

Discuss measuring, ask the children for their understanding of measurement. Why do we do it? How do we do it? What do the children know is measured? What can we measure in the outdoor classroom? Take some ideas, remember that despite your planning you could ask the children to carry out their own measuring task and discuss it with you, rather than follow the planned activity.

Explain that we can measure things by comparing them with others, and model showing a stick that is longer than another one and a child who is shorter than the adult.

Suggest that we may light a fire at the end of this session. What will we need? The children will need to go to collect sticks in order to light the fire. Does anyone know what size sticks we will need first?

Tell the children they are to collect a bundle of sticks that are as long as their hand and thinner than their finger. Demonstrate.

When they have gathered their first bundle explain the next bundle needs to be as long as their elbow to their finger tip and as thin as their finger. The final bundle needs to be as long as their arm and as wide as their finger. As the children gather their sticks, encourage them to try to tie them in a bundle.

When all children have returned with several bundles ask them to help you put them in order, shortest to longest. Which will be needed first, second, third?

Lay out the fire and light it. In turn ask the children to approach the fire with the bundle of sticks they think you should use next. Do the others agree they have selected the right bundle? Why/why not?

At the end of the session put out the fire safely.

Key Stage 1 extension activity

While the fire is lighting, ask the children to each find a stick that they can tie onto the washing line. Are all the sticks the same length? How can we make them hang from shortest to longest? What are the problems associated with this (length of string/ size of knot)?

Key questions

Why are some children's bundles longer than others? Does the size of the child make a difference?

Do we always have to compare things to make measurements or can we use particular tools to help us? What tools and equipment would be helpful?

Why does the fire need the smaller sticks first? What would happen if we only used bigger sticks?

Adults

Encourage the children to check the size of their sticks by putting the ends of two sticks together and checking the other end to compare the lengths.

Discuss how the skill of measuring can be important in every day lives. What else needs measuring?

Support with the physical aspect of tying the bundles together.

Remember that it doesn't matter if the children carry out their own task; support their play as required with praise and encouragement.

Success criteria

By the end of the session all children will have been introduced to the idea of non standard measurement. They will have collected appropriately sized sticks and been able to make their own decision about the suitability for fire lighting. The children will have made comparisons and bundled sticks according to size and length.

Photo 3.6 Ordering stick bundles according to size

Activity 3: Making lattice fence panels for weaving

This week the children will be making a lattice fence panel to start creating a wind break in the outdoor classroom. It would be useful if you were able to show either a completed one or some photos.

Teaching opportunities

Recap measuring from the previous visit. What were we measuring and how were we doing it? Explain that this time they will be measuring for a different purpose and that the measurement will be longer and approximate.

Show the children one long stick, approximately 1m. Ask them to find similar size sticks and bring them to you. Remind children about carrying long sticks (hold it beside them, at one end and pull it behind them).

Measure the sticks – which is longest/shortest? Which is the fattest/thinnest? You will need four sticks that are similar length and thickness. Ask the children to tie them into a square. You may have to demonstrate lashing the sticks together and ensure each is tied off.

Other thinner sticks should be tied to the square to make a lattice pattern.

The children will need to collect greenery and smaller branches suitable for weaving. All of these should be approximately the size of the lattice. If we want the fence panels to blend in, what types of materials will be good for weaving? What will happen to greenery over a period of time, does it matter?

Key Stage 1 extension activities

Can the children work out the optimum length of string they need for the lashings and create a measure for others to follow? For example, as long as their arm, or as long as their stick?

Introduce a metre rule and explain that the sticks should all be a similar length. If the sticks are too long, help the children to saw them down to size.

Key questions

How can you make the sticks shorter?

How will you know how long your string needs to be to tie the sticks together? Challenge the children to find out and make a non standard measurement to follow in future. Can they explain how this will help them?

Adults

Ensure the children are measuring the sticks carefully, with the two ends together. Encourage appropriate vocabulary: longer, shorter, fatter, thinner, etc.

Challenge the children to tie the sticks themselves, offering support only when the children have been trying or have asked for some help. Praise and encourage even the smallest attempts.

Use praise and encouragement, be supportive of all attempts and value a child's ideas and play.

Demonstrate weaving the greenery through, but allow the children time to explore what happens if they don't follow a pattern. Do not discourage children if they are attempting alternative ways, encourage their initiative and discuss whether their idea works.

Success criteria

All children will have attempted to measure using either non standard or standard measures. The children will have discussed how to work out the correct length of string they will need for each tie. Children will have used mathematically appropriate language and will recognize why it is important to be reasonably accurate with their measurements. They will be beginning to consider how they can be more accurate.

Key Stage 1 children will have had a chance to explore a metre rule and will have an understanding of how long a metre is. All children will have used simple tools to saw wood and cut greenery; they will have attempted to make a lashing and there will be some successfully completed fence panels.

Activity 4: Patterns and colours in the natural world

This session gives the children an opportunity to explore colour and pattern in the outdoor classroom. Children will have a chance to gather and use the natural materials they find around them. They will first need to make some choices about the kinds of things they want to collect; it may be leaves, petals, fir cones, bark, feathers, etc.

Teaching opportunities

When the children have gathered their materials they can sort them into baskets according to their properties. The children should be able to create their own categories – hard, soft, round, long, brown, green, etc. Using these materials the children can make simple patterns, repeated patterns, pictures and shapes on the ground. Depending on the materials collected the children may like to stick their pattern onto double-sided sticky tape on a piece of card. They should be able to discuss their choices and describe their patterns. They can take photos of their work to print and display back in the setting.

Encourage the children to share their thinking and their work with others, recognizing other children's good decisions and pattern making.

Key Stage 1 extension activities

Can the children make a pattern that is symmetrical? Are there problems associated with this, such as the stones being different sizes, or the leaves being different shapes? Give the children a small mirror and suggest they make half a pattern and then use the mirror to show it as symmetrical. Use the mirror to explore in the outdoor classroom. Can they find any leaves or flowers that are symmetrical? Take some photos to share back in the setting.

Key questions

Why did they sort their objects in that way? What are the similarities and differences?

Can you explain your pattern to me? Can you make it more complicated by adding an extra item?

Can you show me what makes your pattern symmetrical?

Adults

Some children will need support to collect and sort their objects, but allow the child to explore sorting for themselves, whilst also trying to explain their thinking behind their decisions.

Use praise and encouragement throughout the session, supporting children following the task and those creating their own play. Introduce the appropriate language for describing and sorting and help the child to use the correct vocabulary at the appropriate times.

Use the key questions to challenge the children and encourage more learning and help the children to share what they have been doing with others around them. Perhaps they could evaluate each other's decisions and patterns.

Success criteria

Children will have had an opportunity to collect and sort a range of natural materials into categories according to their properties. They will have had a chance to discuss their decisions and explain their reasoning with both adults and other children.

Most children will have created simple and repeating patterns using their materials and some will have made symmetrical shapes and patterns. They will have recorded their work using a digital camera and will have the chance to view and print their work in the classroom. Some children will have explored symmetry using mirrors and may have found leaves and flowers that are symmetrical. Children will have had an opportunity to evaluate and discuss other children's work.

Conclusion

Topic work is particularly well suited to the outdoor classroom, it allows for some ordered and more formal learning to take place in the classroom to support the more child-led activities taking place outside. Topic work overlaps and becomes cross-curricular without too much effort and it will meet the needs of the majority of children. Using the outdoor classroom in such a way ensures its continuing development, and very quickly a bank of ideas can be built up and developed across all year groups.

As practitioners become more confident, ideas become embedded and children become more able and independent in the outdoor space. Certainly those teachers using the outdoors regularly for this style of learning find that the inspiration created outdoors generates a high standard of work throughout the project.

4 How do activities and experiences in the outdoor classroom fit in the curriculum?

Introduction

The purpose of this chapter is to demonstrate how play and learning in the outdoor classroom can be planned to link with the work going on inside the classroom on a daily basis. It models how a combination of different planning styles can work alongside each other to provide the best learning experiences. It will emphasize how child/adult-led and child/adult-initiated activities can work successfully together in both a reception class and into Key Stage 1. The chapter will detail some of the ways that the good practice developed in the Early Years, of learning through play, can be continued into Year 1 and 2, whilst still covering the important and essential aspects of the National Curriculum.

As with all planning it is important to note that it would need to be adapted to suit the needs of the children and adults you are working with. It would be particularly important to ensure the inclusion of all children in the group, especially those with additional learning and behavioural needs. The planning in this chapter does include some additional notes added during and after each session.

In my experience it would appear that making outdoor learning opportunities fit within the relevant curriculum is often cited as the reason for inadequate or infrequent provision, across all settings. It is the most-quoted reason given for not being able to sustain outdoor learning regularly or for more than a few weeks at a time. The examples of planning used in this chapter will give indicators that highlight how simple it is to continue the indoor learning process outside. It is a similar planning process used to provide good outdoor learning experiences in many of the settings I have visited and will help to model how learning outside should be a part of the initial stages of planning, rather than an add-on if it feels appropriate.

The modern trend to plan extensively and have set objectives for every moment of the school day means that learning experiences can be stifled, limiting exploration and impulsive learning in children of all ages. Often the resulting problem is a lack of lessons that are cross-curricular, and independent play experiences are limited. Some schools prefer to teach discrete subject areas, which will ultimately lead to anxieties about the way the outdoor classroom is used. It takes a brave and experienced teacher to recognize what aspect of learning is taking place and to value it more highly than the planned experiences that perhaps are not taking place. Does it matter if we return to our planning and rewrite what actually happened and describe what those children actually learned? Rather than seeing this as a negative experience, it should be celebrated that the children were able to learn about things that inspired them, that they met their own individual needs and developed their own skills of observation and investigation. Even the best and most comprehensive set of plans cannot take into consideration the learning styles, stages of development and interests of all the children in the group. Child-led but adult-supported activities can do that. The adult needs to learn to be a supporter to the child; someone to advise, give hands-on support and, through good questioning, take the child's thinking to the next level. Such experiences are challenging to plan for and it often becomes even harder to ensure that they are carried out. If an adult is particularly concerned about meeting their own outcomes, then learning outside becomes fraught with worries about unfulfilled planning and unmet objectives. An anxious teacher or practitioner will not help the children to feel free to learn in their own way and will lead to over-planned lessons, over-anxious children and unachieved objectives.

However despite my belief that we must be led by the children, I also recognize that if we are to be able to use the outdoor classroom on a regular basis, throughout all year groups, with the support of colleagues and government inspectors, then we must show how it fits with our curriculum.

The Early Years Foundation Stage (EYFS) (2007/2011)

This document is an extensive statutory document that seeks to cover all aspects of a young child's learning and development until the age of five years. This curriculum has to be provided by all maintained schools and early years' providers in the state, private and voluntary sectors in the UK. This includes maintained schools, pre-schools and nurseries, as well as childminders, play schemes and children's centres. The curriculum was devised to ensure all children were given opportunities to learn through play regardless of their background, ability and additional needs. It also stipulates that all children should have opportunities to play outside on a daily basis and as such settings are now looking for ways to extend outdoor play, in particular free flow between the indoors and the outdoors. Whilst this is not sufficient to count as an outdoor classroom it is a change in attitude that will, over time, help practitioners to be more confident in using this as a learning space. Because the EYFS is such an extensive curriculum it is relatively easy for an experienced practitioner to make links to learning opportunities outside and to be confident that the children in their care are learning appropriately. In fact there are actually very few goals that cannot be met in the outdoor classroom just as adequately as they are within the setting walls.

The EYFS contains specific areas of learning and each subject has its own set of small steps and goals for the children to be working towards during their most formative years. The steps are in age-appropriate stages and it is anticipated that by the time the children leave the Foundation Stage they will have met the majority of these goals in preparation for beginning their learning in the National Curriculum.

Opportunities for developing personal, social and emotional skills are widespread in the outdoor classroom. There are new challenges, it's a more risky environment, and there are opportunities for small-group tasks, decision making and cooperative work. These skills lead well into helping the children develop the skills of sharing, listening, taking turns and respecting others' ideas. In fact, it is often noted by practitioners that the children who find leading and decision making difficult in the classroom can excel in the outdoor classroom. Often the children who are the quietest inside become the leaders and decision makers outside, and those who dominate play indoors frequently take a step back once play is taken outside and perhaps out of their comfort zone.

Finding out about our world

The children are expected to learn about their world, finding out about many aspects of learning and everyday life, such as living things, observing features of the local environment, developing curiosity and understanding their own likes and dislikes. Opportunities to fulfil these goals are endless outside, in particular when the child leads play and they are able to follow their own ideas and explore with freedom and independence. Taking children regularly to the same space allows them to make comparisons and note changes on each visit, so without any formal learning experiences the child is finding out about their environment, their likes and dislikes. Using cameras to record progress and work carried out provides evidence of the child's learning; however giving the camera to the child encourages them to record their own learning, whilst fulfilling some aspects of the ICT expectations. Discussing how food can be cooked around or over a fire will help the children to recognize that in some countries this is normal behaviour. Teaching respect for other cultures through the introduction of how people live, types of homes and ways of preparing food can be made quite simple if the outdoor classroom can be utilized for some of the teaching.

Physical development

Physical development, an important element of the curriculum, includes moving safely, showing awareness of others and of space, as well as using a range of tools and equipment. Children have to learn to negotiate the unexpected, fallen trees, muddy paths, etc. Such activities all lead to improved balance and coordination. In the outdoors, children can make bigger movements, run faster and further, they can climb, jump, balance and crouch. All these contribute to well-developed gross motor skills, reducing clumsiness and poor coordination. In the outdoor classroom, through the supported use of basic tools such as saws and pen knives the children are able to improve their fine motor skills, whilst increasing the range of activities they are becoming confident in. There is little doubt that this is an area of the Early Years' curriculum that can be comfortably met through the use of the outdoors and with skilled and supportive staff to ensure that fine and gross motor skills are developed and progression is made.

Communicating with others

Communication, taught through the area of Speech, Language and Literacy provides children with opportunities to explore the many interlinked elements of reading, writing and speaking. Using the outdoor classroom can make situations real, and there is no greater inspiration for speech and language development than the excitement that can be generated from regular visits to the outdoor classroom. Children learn to speak to each other and to the adults with them. They have opportunities to ask questions, explain their findings, share their news and try out new words. Listening and responding to others become a crucial part of working successfully in a group and sharing in others' excitement needs communication skills, whether they are verbal or physical. Using the outdoor classroom as a place to be inspired, to share stories and make up new ones, creates endless and frequently changing backdrops from which to begin. There is no end of characters that can be hiding in the woods, living in the rabbit holes or cooking their lunch around a fire! The children can act out well-known characters and use the descriptive words they have heard in storytelling: the big bad wolf, the dark forest, the long winding path.

Through very simple activities we can demonstrate the conventions of language, sorting objects that start with a particular initial sound, creating sentences and story openings with familiar words, 'once upon a time', 'in the dark wood', etc. The children's use of language can be extensive and their vocabulary can be enhanced by the adults working alongside them, in exactly the same way as we teach in a classroom.

There is nothing wrong with taking classroom provisions outside in order to write or mark make, using large paint brushes, charcoaled wood, sticks and leaves. Making the learning different and interesting is likely to be successful and encourage children to participate and to try. Succeeding in the outdoor environment is more likely to ensure the children return to the classroom positive about their ability and willing to have a go at something they may have been avoiding!

Mathematics

The teaching of numeracy and mathematics is just as easily fitted into work in the outdoor classroom. Children can use the natural materials around them to make comparisons between size, shape and colour. They can explore pattern and shape, using words to describe the irregular shape of leaves or the symmetrical pattern on a butterfly. Using sticks and branches children can find out about mathematical concepts such as larger and smaller, heavier and lighter. Once introduced to the idea that a stick can be shorter or longer than their arm, children will spend endless sessions looking for a stick that fulfils the criteria. Usually if it is shorter than their arm, they can play with it. We have a rule that if a stick is longer than their arm then it should not be played with. It can be picked up correctly by two children and used for a specific purpose, it cannot be waved around during free play. It's amazing how quickly the children, in particular the boys, learn how to measure sticks if they know they can go on to use it in their play!

Developing imagination through creative play

Learning about creativity and imaginative play allows children time for exploration and discovery in the outdoor classroom. Children can be shown how to use the materials around them to make two- and three-dimensional pictures and sculptures. Once the children have had some inspiration and a little excitement and praise from the adults they are able to continue to be creative in their own individual way. The ideas are limitless and however hard the practitioner tries, we will never come up with all the ideas the children will think of! Taking photos and making displays back in the classroom will inspire the children to continue to be creative, and on subsequent visits it is likely other children will be exploring similar activities and ideas for themselves.

Introducing music into the outdoor environment is a new concept for many children, and indeed the adults working with them. But it is easy to knock two sticks together to make a sound, or to wave a handful of leaves to hear them rustle. Finding materials that make sounds and sorting them – 'do they rattle?', 'do they have to be knocked together?' – is a simple idea that will get children looking at their environment in a different way. I have witnessed more than one 'rock' band, gathered around a tree with a selection of sticks and stones, making random noises they tell me is music! Utilize this excitement and add words and write songs. Ask the children how we can make a space that is for music making, where will it be and what will it need?

For a new dimension to play in the outdoor classroom, show children how they can make camouflage from the things around them. Discuss what they would need to hide from the wolf; what colours will be the best for hiding in and why?

This flexible and creative curriculum is the reason why so many early years' settings and reception classes have been among the first to initiate learning in the outdoors, to create outdoor classrooms and to instil the use of the Forest School ethos into their environment.

Developing outdoor learning beyond the early years

One of the biggest issues facing schools that have developed this style of learning, where young children are receiving a rich and varied curriculum, with diverse learning environments and experiences in their reception class, is how it can be continued into Key Stage 1. Currently all too many children are having fantastic, rich experiences in their formative years that sadly stop when they move to Year 1. With such a focus on transition between key stages it is now important to consider how teachers in Years 1 and 2 can continue with the good practice being developed lower down the school.

With the research showing that the outdoor classroom can improve self-esteem and confidence, as well as help behaviour problems, it should now be a priority that schools consider how to maintain the use of the outdoor classroom through their school.

When we start to compare the EYFS curriculum with that of Key Stage 1, it becomes clear why the process of learning in an outdoor environment has taken longer to embed in the latter. With the assessment of children's ability becoming so high profile from this age onwards, teachers feel far less empowered to take chances with their children's learning, preferring to stay with what they can be certain will ensure good results at the end of the year and at the end of key stage assessments.

To address this obvious reduction in outdoor play, some areas in the country are beginning to consider how outdoor learning can successfully be continued throughout the school. Recognizing that this approach can develop confidence and self-esteem, which in turn is likely to raise standards, is a good step in the right direction. However, that still leaves many teachers wondering how they can afford to take time away from formal learning for these more natural and child-led experiences.

Considering the outdoor classroom as an extension to the indoors is a good place to start. Hopefully the children have explored and played in this environment in their reception year and the initial excitement of something new is less intense each week! This should enable some more planned and cross-curricular experiences to successfully take place. Fitting these opportunities into the Key Stage 1 National Curriculum might take more thought than in the early years, but it is certainly manageable and a creative thinker and their class of excited learners should have few problems.

The National Curriculum

Of course the National Curriculum currently has specific and individual subject areas. Literacy, numeracy, science and ICT being known as the core subjects, and these also have more emphasis placed on them in assessment at the end of each key stage. Because of this pressure, these areas are taught discretely almost exclusively in a classroom, with just the occasional visit outside to support a particular aspect of the current learning taking place.

Literacy

With the importance of good speaking and listening skills becoming more high profile, it is easy to see how the same skills developed in the early years can be extended and developed to the next level, whilst outside. Listening, questioning, retelling stories, acting out stories and improving the use of adjectives and exciting vocabulary cover large amounts of the objectives to be taught in Key Stage 1 literacy. Many teachers have also noticed that providing exciting and unusual stimulation will often result in improved writing back in the classroom, giving the children a broader range of experiences to draw on. Is there any reason why phonics cannot be reinforced outside, why sentence structure should be done sitting at a table or even why quiet and shared reading cannot be done sitting in a log circle in an outdoor classroom?

Numeracy

Numeracy can be just as creative. Using real life contexts is exciting and stimulating, counting and adding together real objects, measuring real trees and branches, using positional language, looking for shapes in the world around us and identifying symmetry in nature are just a few ways that numeracy can be taken outside. Given these 'real' experiences children will find ways of solving everyday problems in other environments, and numeracy will no longer be something that can only be learnt in a classroom.

Science

Some aspects of science are more obviously linked to outdoor learning and in terms of teaching outdoors are an easier link to make. Environments, habitats, mini-beasts and growing all lend themselves to outdoor learning and exploring in the natural environment. Materials and their uses can also be successfully taught outside. What fabric will be waterproof? Which materials are natural and man-made? With the focus being on the teaching and use of investigative skills, children have opportunities to devise their own methods for finding out similarities and differences, for explaining habitats and setting up a simple experiment to determine which material would make the best shelter for their den. Recording their work can be done back in the classroom, where the children will be animated from their physical hands-on experiences. Using photos to prompt responses helps the children to recall the method, the results and the evaluation processes.

Information, communications and technology (ICT)

ICT is also easy to integrate into planning through the use of cameras, videos and recording instruments. Collecting data from the outdoor classroom that can be brought back and manipulated makes it real for the children. The children can see their own photos on the school website, make their own animation from their stills and edit their own videos. They are able to take ownership of the whole exercise and as a result will be proud of their work and keen to continue with more opportunities in future lessons. It is very clear that learning about the weather and recording information about the weather, rainfall, wind speed and daily temperatures is most likely to be exciting when done first-hand. Children are able to use a digital microscope and a laptop to make observations about the outdoors whilst still in the environment, provoking a better use of vocabulary.

Personal, social and health education

The essential skills taught in personal, social and health education continue to develop from those in the early years. Respect for themselves and others, likes and dislikes, fair and unfair, sharing opinions and views and working with others take a high priority throughout school and can be learnt and reinforced with ease in the outdoor classroom. Children learn to cooperate with each other and work outside their comfort zone; to explain their ideas to others and to listen to each other's input.

Summary

Teaching in the outdoors need not be any more complicated than teaching indoors, in fact once you are in the habit of using the space regularly, the opportunities are endless and are continually developing. Justifying your time spent in the outdoor classroom should not be difficult and the results of such opportunities will be clear for all. Starting to think of all that happens in the outdoor classroom as learning, knowing that it is likely to cover objectives you might not have considered, and being prepared to change your plans because of a frog sitting beside the pond, or a heavy snow fall, is a good place for any practitioner to start. Relax and enjoy the learning with your children and be inspired by their enthusiasm and excitement!

The following series of lessons will highlight how a topic started in the classroom can be transferred to an experience in the outdoor classroom. As with all planning I have annotated and altered each activity after it has taken place. There are assessment notes, and future learning has been included for my own information.

Early Years Foundation Stage
Communication and Language (Listening and Attention)

Objectives
- children can give their attention to what is being said to them and can respond appropriately;
- children listen attentively in a range of situations.

Adult-led/classroom activity
Circle Time (*Children needed time to reflect on our circle time rules.*)
Generate a discussion about the children's favourite places in the outdoor classroom. (*Photos were useful as prompts.*) Model how to speak and listen in a small group: level of voice, eye contact, body language, facial expression, etc.
Encourage children to take turns to share their views and describe their favourite place. Ask some questions and model waiting for an answer and clarifying the question if necessary.
Provide opportunities for all children to take part, if they choose to.

Child-initiated/classroom activity
Role play/shelter building
The children should have access to a range of props for supporting their play. These should include fabric, pegs, string and rope, pictures of dens and tents.
Allow the children to lead the play themselves, but support if necessary and play alongside them. Encourage the children to share their ideas with each other and listen for good communication skills. Praise children who respond to others' suggestions and work well together. Don't get involved in the decision making, this is a child-initiated activity. (*The children needed more intervention than I had planned for. Once started most of the groups became more independent throughout the session. Some children needed adult support and encouragement throughout.*)

Adult-initiated/child-led activity in the outdoor classroom
Building a tepee
Read a story about Native American Indians, and discuss where they lived.
Provide the children with a range of materials necessary for building a tepee: fabric, tarpaulin, rope, sticks, etc. Pictures of completed tepees are useful, and allow the children copies of the book to use for retelling purposes.
Encourage the children to work together to collect their materials and make plans together for making and building their tepee.
Praise children who are listening and responding to each other, asking and answering questions and generally working well in a group. (*Children were clearly more independent in this task, generally they achieved well. Pictures of tepees were useful.*)

Success criteria
Children have met the objectives in more than one activity, in particular demonstrating their skills in activities that are child-initiated and child-led. Children have improved their listening skills, and listen and respond through appropriate questioning. They are able to share ideas, respond to others' suggestions and make their own adaptations through discussion in a small group.

<table>
<tr><td colspan="1" align="center">

Key Stage 1
Communication and Language (Speaking and Listening)

</td></tr>
</table>

Objectives • to join in as members of a group, pupils should be taught to take turns in speaking; • to listen, understand and respond to others, pupils should be taught to ask questions to clarify their understanding.
Adult-led/classroom activity Circle Time – Where is your favourite place in the outdoor classroom? (*I actually started the lesson with a short slide show using pictures taken on previous visits to the outdoor classroom.*) Ask children to recap the rules we need for speaking in small groups, turn taking, one person speaking at a time, etc. During this circle it is important that the teacher speaks clearly and demonstrates good listening skills and in return expects children to behave in the same way. Introduce the idea of asking questions to find out more information. Remind the children about closed and open questions. Ask the children to try and use a question in response to someone else's statement. Can they consider what question starter will ensure they get the most detail – open or closed? (*This lesson followed closely after a series of lessons about questioning, children would have found this hard without that input.*)
Child-led/classroom activity Give the children an opportunity to continue their discussions in small groups. Place question starters on the tables and allow the children to discuss and question independently. Explain that you want to hear the children asking open questions. Encourage the children to write the questions they are using on postcards. At the end of the session share good examples of open questioning. (*This lesson was very successful, children were engaged and on task. Question cards were a useful prompt.*)
Adult-initiated/child-led activity in the outdoor classroom Discuss making a shelter that will help to keep your group dry if it rains. What kind of shelters do the children know how to make? Take suggestions. In small groups ask the children to collect the resources they need and to build themselves a shelter that will keep out the rain. (*We recapped work done in science about materials before starting.*) Encourage discussion and questioning within the group. When someone makes a suggestion ask someone in the group to challenge their idea using an open question. For example, why should we use that rope? What will happen if we use those branches? (*For future reference, children found questioning others difficult.*)
Success criteria Children are comfortable both questioning and challenging others' ideas and being questioned and challenged. (*They found this difficult, will need more input to meet these criteria.*) Within their discussion they are respectful and understanding of others' views and opinions, showing good manners and applying rules of conversations. Children know how to ask questions that will ensure the most informative answer. Children are able to apply their knowledge to other situations, without adult encouragement.

Early Years Foundation Stage *Creativity and Imagination*

Objectives

By the end of the series of lessons children will have had opportunities:

- to improve their fine motor skills and hand–eye coordination, across a range of activities;
- to use texture and colour to design and make their own creations.

Adult-led/classroom activity

Children should be given a specific task to complete that involves opportunities to develop their fine motor skills. (*Linked to Autumn topic.*)

For example, to draw, cut out, collage and paint an autumn tree. Encourage the children to cut carefully around the lines, model taking care and cutting safely. They should choose the medium they want to use to colour their tree in autumn colours. (*Early in the school year and children found making the choice of medium quite hard; some examples would have helped.*)

Alternatively use clay to make a hedgehog. Show the children how they can make the clay into a ball and flatten the bottom. They should pinch out a nose shape and using scissors carefully cut into the back to create spikes. (*Brilliant fun, we poked sticks in to make prickles.*)

Child-led/classroom activity

Set up the creative table with a variety of paints, crayons, chalks, collage materials, etc. Leave some examples of completed works for the children to use as inspiration if they need it. Throughout the session ensure the children have access to the materials they need and get support if they ask for it. (*With less structure and expectation the children managed this task very well.*)

Adult-initiated/child-led activity in the outdoor classroom

Show the children a selection of hanging decorations made with natural materials. Explain that they can make their own using materials they can find in the outdoor classroom and some additional natural items supplied by you.

Provide a wide range of materials and tools, peelers, secateurs, scissors, string, cork, tree bark, fir cones, etc. (*Ensure adult support around the tools.*)

Success criteria

Children have experienced a range of opportunities in the classroom that have helped them transfer their skills to the outdoor classroom. Most children will become more confident using familiar tools and will happily attempt to use new implements, although they are likely to need some support. Children are able to carry out tasks independently and successfully. They will be proud of their achievements. (*The outcomes were very varied in all tasks, but the children did particularly well in the less adult–led tasks.*)

Key Stage 1 Art and Design
Objectives By the end of the series of lessons children will have had opportunities: • to explore colour, pattern, texture, shape form and space in two and three dimensions; • to represent their observations, in a form of their choice; • to design and make images and artefacts.
Adult-led/classroom activity As with Early Years planning, children will need to be given a set task to begin this series of lessons. (*Our focus was the changing seasons.*) In line with the theme about the outdoors, children were asked to make a three-dimensional autumn tree. Resources should include boxes, tubes, card, paper, tissue and several ways of fixing the items, tape, glue, staples, etc. Encourage the children to share ideas that work, and make suggestions about how they can improve their own work. (*Allow more time than expected for feedback, they were very proud of their work and we ran into another session.*)
Child-led/classroom activity Following the previous session, children should be given a wide selection of materials to continue with the theme of designing and making using different mediums and tools. (*We continued the changing seasons theme.*) They should be encouraged to create using their own three-dimensional ideas. (*Some children sketched their ideas first.*) There is a need for children to display some accuracy in their work. Support should be given as required, but suggestions should be limited, allowing children to make their own decisions and follow their own ideas through. Careful questioning will allow children to make these choices more considered. (*The less able children needed to be helped with decision making, limiting options was the most successful way of dealing with this.*)
Adult-initiated/child-led activity in the outdoor classroom Encourage children to reflect on their previous dimensional structures. Are there any lessons that can be used to support learning today in the outdoor classroom? (*The children that sketched in the classroom were keen to do this again.*) Explain that today the resources are natural and can be collected from the outdoor classroom. Children should have a range of tools, string and rope and if necessary additional natural materials to supplement those available. The children will design and make their own mobile/decoration using the resources around them. Adult support will be necessary when the children are using tools.
Success criteria Children will have had experience of working with a wide range of materials to produce their own work. They will have used several methods to join items, and will know why some work better than others. They will understand that some materials are best suited to specific uses and will be able to design and make their own decoration.

<table>
<tr><td colspan="1">

Early Years Foundation Stage
Mathematics, Numbers

Objectives
By the end of the series of lessons children will have had opportunities:
* to show curiosity about numbers through play experiences;
* to recognize and order numbers to 10;
* to estimate a number of objects and check quantities by counting up to 10.

</td></tr>
</table>

Adult-led/classroom activity
Using a selection of natural resources, set up activities that will help the children to learn to count to 10 accurately. Demonstrate how lining the objects up can help us to count accurately.
Collect a small selection of objects and ask for estimates up to 10. Take and record answers. Count to check how many items you have and check who has the most accurate guess. Repeat several times with different numbers.
Using large-scale number cards count the correct number of items onto each card. *(This is a useful assessment exercise for counting accurately to 10.)*
Introduce children to simple dice and counting games, encourage 1:1 correspondence. *(Children were unfamiliar with the games and needed support.)*

Child-led/classroom activity
Provide opportunities for the children to play counting games independently. Use spinners with numbers to 10 and dice with numbers to 6.
Within play activities ensure the children have access to counters, toys, number cards and number lines.
Outside, encourage children to use playground number lines, hopscotch grids and number tiles for play. *(Outside was popular and some children continued into playtime.)*

Adult-initiated/child-led activity in the outdoor classroom
Ask the children to consider what they can count and collect in the outdoor classroom. Take ideas and ask the children to look for a specific number of their item – sticks, stones, leaves, etc. Ask them to check their counting by lining up the objects and counting, 1:1.
Take a small handful of sticks and estimate how many sticks you are holding. Repeat asking the children for their estimates. Whose estimate was the most accurate?
Show the children a number card and ask them to look for that number of sticks. When they return they should check they have the right number and then tie them into a bundle. How many bundles have we got? Count together. *(Some children needed help tying the bundles; others were able to support their friends.)*
Repeat with a different number card.
When children are more adept at tying they may like to tie their sticks into a mobile or hanging decoration. Children can continue to collect and tie their sticks, each time choosing a new number card and counting before tying.

Success criteria
Children are becoming familiar with numbers to 10. Most children can say the numbers in order, some will recognize and order number cards correctly.
Children are familiar with the term 'estimate' and can make reasonable estimations using numbers to 10. They are beginning to understand how near their guess is to the correct number. *(Children transferred their classroom learning into the outdoors very easily.)*

Key Stage 1
Mathematics, Numbers

Objectives

By the end of the series of lessons children will have had opportunities:
- to count reliably to 20;
- to recognize that when objects are rearranged the number stays the same;
- to count accurately in multiples of 10.

Adult-led/classroom activity

Begin the session with some quick games involving numbers to 20: ordering cards, finding the correct number of items and number recognition opportunities. *(This needed good preparation and a lot of readily available resources.)*

Explain to the children that you will be using a 100 square and ask them to look for patterns of numbers within the square. Discuss how each line has 10 numbers and that each of the subsequent lines below has the same number in the units column. Show how the number square can help us to count in 10s.

Ask the children to complete a number square that has some blanks. Explain that they can use the patterns to help them complete accurately.

When the children have completed their square they can use a spinner (1–10) and counters to play a simple counting game. When they spin 10 do they need to count each square, or is there a short cut?

Child-led/classroom activity

Provide a selection of activities that will consolidate the children's learning about counting in 10s.

Dice and counters.

Place value cards that need ordering.

Spinners (1–10) and number grid style games.

Number cards (1–20)

Interactive white board games.

(Children needed some introduction to these activities, but were independent playing them.)

Adult-initiated/child-led activity in the outdoor classroom

Continue with the theme counting to 20 and multiples of 10.

Using the need for dry kindling as an excuse, ask the children to gather some sticks. They will need to be carefully counted into bundles of 10, before being tied together.

Each bundle can be laid on the ground in a row. How many bundles do we need to make 100 sticks? Repeat for different numbers. Encourage counting in multiples of 10. *(This visual way worked very well for the less able and I reinforced classroom learning in a similar way in subsequent lesson.)*

Success criteria

Children will have practised counting to 10, 20. They will know how a number square can help them to count in multiples of 10. They will have used a range of materials to help them rehearse counting in 10s.

Some children will be able to apply counting in multiples of 10 to some simple everyday problems.

<table>
<tr><td colspan="1">

Early Years Foundation Stage
Understanding the World

Objectives
By the end of the series of lessons children will have had opportunities:
- to talk about the features of their own immediate environment and how environments might vary from one another;
- to make observations of animals and plants and explain why some things occur, and talk about changes, including in simple experiments.

Adult-led/classroom activity
Using photos and Internet sites, look at some of the creatures you might expect to live in the outdoor classroom and some that won't. (*Initially use pictures that are very extreme, for example tigers and rabbits.*) Help the children to name the ones that are less familiar. Which creatures do the children think they are most likely to find in our school?
Provide pictures of the creatures for the children to sort into categories. For example, will find at school, will not find at school. (*They enjoyed this task; it was useful to have more than one set of pictures.*)

Child-led/classroom activity
Provide a range of activities that will support this series of lessons.
Mini-beast cards and name cards for pairing.
Collage table with example picture of mini-beasts and local creatures.
Den-building materials and creature masks.
Wormery or ant farm, with magnifying glasses.
(*Children needed some introduction to these resources, but coped without too much intervention.*)

Adult-initiated/child-led activity in the outdoor classroom
Provide opportunities and resources for the children to go bug hunting.
Identification charts, magnifiers, clipboards and pencils.
Small yoghurt pots, fruit and trowels for making sunken bug traps. (*Make sure the children empty these traps before leaving.*)
Cameras, handheld digital microscope and laptop for immediate playback.
Encourage questions about why they are finding bugs in specific places, what the bug may eat, why it has certain features. (*We found unidentifiable bugs, so took photos to bring back and check online.*)

Success criteria
Children will have organized creatures into local and not local categories. They will have explored how creatures survive, what they eat, where they live. Some children will have considered what may threaten the creatures in their environment and how we can help them.
Children will be able to name some of the most common mini-beasts and will know how to use ID charts to help them with less common creatures.
(*Finding an unknown bug was very exciting for the children, they said they were explorers!*)

</td></tr>
</table>

Key Stage 1
Science

Objectives

By the end of the series of lessons children will have had opportunities:
- to find out about the different kinds of animals in the local environment;
- to group living things according to observable similarities and differences;
- to use first-hand experience and simple information sources to answer questions.

Adult-led/classroom activity

Start the lesson looking at and identifying creatures and mini-beasts that will be found in the outdoor classroom. Ask the children to talk about the creatures' features and what they already know about where they will be living. (*This was very familiar to the children; a challenge would have been to use a key for ID purposes.*)
Explain that all creatures face hazards from their environment, and with the children make a list of the things that may affect a small creature.

Child-led/classroom activity

Provide independent activities to support the previous session.
Mini-beast picture cards and hazard words for matching and discussing how that creature avoids that hazard. For example a woodlouse under a rock is safe from birds.
Mini-beast and habitat pictures for pairing.
Identification charts and photos. ID keys already set up on computers.
Junk modelling, collage, painting and mini-beast pictures for ideas. (*Children making junk bugs were able to talk about the features of the bug, wings to fly fast and a hard shell.*)

Adult-initiated/child-led activity in the outdoor classroom

Children should be able to work independently in the following tasks.
Bug hunting and recording their findings on a simple chart or table. This should record what the creature is, where it was found and what one of its hazards may be.
Identification charts, magnifiers and a camera.
Sketch books and pencils, crayons.
(*The children were really independent in this task and completed it really well. They made good suggestions about why the creatures lived in their homes.*)

Success criteria

Children will have successfully found mini-beasts around their school. They will know the names of the most common and be able to discuss why they live in their particular habitat. They will know that all creatures face hazards either from nature or from humans and will know how some of the creatures protect themselves. Children will be becoming independent in their learning, questioning and identifying the answers through a range of sources.

Conclusion

This chapter has shown how simple it is to create opportunities for outdoor play in everyday teaching. The activities are deliberately simple, not dependent on vast quantities of expensive resources; neither do they require extensive preparation. They are straightforward and manageable alongside the very busy and structured timetables most teachers are dealing with.

Just a little creative thinking will turn an indoor activity into a real-life outdoor play experience. The inspiration that comes from even the briefest outdoor encounter can be inspirational and can add a new dimension to normal, daily teaching. Finding out how many legs a woodlouse has will always be more fun if, before counting, you need to catch and identify the bug and then it needs to stay still. The more it wriggles the more the children will learn. If it scurries under a leaf, they learn it likes the dark, if it curls up they know it has a defence mechanism. They can find this out from a book, but can also confirm their own first-hand observations through an appropriate medium. This approach ensures that the lesson will become more memorable.

Teaching young children to count tangible and visual objects is likely to be more successful. For accurate counting children need to see and feel the objects. Sticks can be lined up, piled up, ordered by size and touched with each number spoken. They can be moved, rearranged, added to and taken from. With the basic skills in counting so vividly reinforced, children are more likely to go on to be more successful when the time comes to record the work they are doing in a more formal way.

While, in the ideal world, children should be able to access outdoor play freely and without restriction, there is also a need to remember that this is not always achievable. In this case any work done outside will make an interesting diversion to the more traditional lessons. When planning a unit of work or building a new topic perhaps it would be helpful if practitioners and teachers added a new area to their planning sheets, labelled 'outdoor classroom'. Teachers are generally conscientious, hardworking and thorough and not many would leave part of a planning sheet unworked. The new 'outdoor classroom' section would soon be filled with inspirational activities and adventurous play opportunities, all of them neatly linked back to the essential work taking place in the classroom.

5 | The outdoor classroom in practice

Introduction

It is important when we are considering how to use the outdoor classroom that we look at other settings and learn from their experiences. This chapter looks at three establishments, working with different age ranges and in varying localities in the UK. Each of these places of learning already has established Forest School style of learning taking place on a regular basis and each one has made its own alterations to the Forest School model to make it work for them and their children in their care.

These three settings began their outdoor learning from the very beginning, finding their way through trial and error until they have arrived at the point they are now at. But none of these places is happy to sit back; each is still working on the sustainability and development of their provision.

Children are asked about what they want to do in their own space, what resources they want, what games they should play and how they should play there. To inspire creativity children use 'talking tubs' to present a selection of photos and objects to share, touch and play with; they are designed to challenge thinking and increase engagement.

Case study: a small rural first school

Mark Church of England First School is a small rural school in Somerset which benefits from large spacious grounds, including a safely fenced pond area and an outdoor classroom. In this instance the phrase 'outdoor classroom' is used in its most sincere sense. The space is natural, has some trees, a good variety of native plants and a large log circle with a fire pit.

In 2004 the outdoor classroom began almost by accident when a teacher at the school stumbled across some unused, naturally wild, land beyond the perimeter fence at the far end of the field. Upon further investigation it was established that this land belonged to the school and it was soon re-fenced to keep the children away from the adjoining ditch. By the following summer the outdoor classroom had been largely cleared of its dense undergrowth and was ready for the children.

The school was able to make use of a teacher who was qualified with the level three Forest School leader award and who was able see the potential and enthuse other members of the school community. A whole-school training day was organized to give all members of staff the chance to learn more about the work that could be carried on in this newly found space. Since its inception two further members of the teaching staff have been awarded the level three Forest School leaders award and a teaching assistant has completed the Forest School key skills training.

It was considered important that all staff working in the school were able to see the benefit of teaching the children in this way in order for the use of the outdoor classroom to be successful and positive for all the participants. The intention being that the space was used across all year groups, weekly throughout the year, involving all members of classroom staff.

Initially the school had few resources specifically put aside for the outdoor classroom, managing on the natural materials readily available within the grounds and occasionally taking additional items from the main school resources. As the area and its use has developed so have the resources, and the school now has a shed within the outdoor classroom that secures the property when not in use.

The planning for each class is carried out by the class teachers and is monitored by the headteacher. Planning sheets were adapted to make allowances for the outdoor classroom and this has helped to give it the same level of priority as other teaching areas in the school. Staff have also commented that having additional space in their planning format ensures they give consideration to their outdoor classroom time whilst planning for the rest of the curriculum. It has become a normal part of planning and teaching in each class. The aim is that every class visits the area weekly for a minimum of either a morning or an afternoon, although as the curriculum becomes busier into Key Stage 2, even the most avid fan of the outdoor classroom finds it hard to make time each week. For the Foundation Stage and Key Stage 1, using the outdoor classroom every week is now embedded and happens regardless of weather. There are a few issues that may affect how and when the space is used, such as high winds and falling branches, lack of available adults or whole-school events. When sessions are missed, teachers try to incorporate them elsewhere in their timetable.

Initially teachers were concerned that not all members of staff would be as enthusiastic as they were about using the area, particularly in the cold and wet, when the ground is muddy and the wind is brisk. But the support staff were equally keen to teach the children outside, and as new members of staff have arrived in school the enthusiasm has spread and there is very little resistance.

In order to reassure the parents that what they wanted to do was safe and would add value to their child's learning, teachers ran workshops inviting interested parties into the area to work alongside their child. From this the school has been able to use keen volunteer parents to ensure adult–child ratios have been maintained in all taught sessions. Induction workshops for parents of new reception children are now part of the process of welcoming new families to the school, and ensuring parents have had this opportunity has reduced the concerns that they may have had as well as provided a chance to discuss the concept and share their worries with teachers. The school has had very little negative feedback since they began using the outdoor classroom.

Children in the school now keep a set of outdoor clothes in their classroom at all times, allowing some flexibility in the timetable. Wellington boots are also stored at school, with most parents happily supplying a pair specifically for school so they do not have to be brought in and out at the end of each term.

Teachers have had to learn to turn a blind eye to the little piles of mud that creep across the carpet and the stack of boots outside the door at the end of the day, although new storage has been added to try to accommodate the extra kit. Staff report that children are more comfortable in old clothes, benefiting from the knowledge that they can get dirty without any consequences. Wet and muddy clothes are dried or sent home to be washed and replaced as soon as possible.

The school is in its sixth year of providing outdoor classroom learning and is seeing the benefits throughout the year groups. Perhaps the most marked difference is in the new reception class, who on their first visits stay close to the adults and need planned and led activities to keep them occupied. By the end of the first term of weekly visits most children are roaming freely, and although they are never far from an adult they do not seem to seek them out so frequently. Whilst activities and opportunities are still planned for and provided, the play and learning is beginning to be led by the children. They are happy to return to previous play and some will explore the same pile of logs on each visit, but they are also confident enough to be looking for new play and will explore more freely. Staff are happy to admit that often the planned activities are abandoned or adapted in order to follow the children's self-initiated play. Working as a team the staff here are able to evaluate the learning that takes place in each session, making links to the curriculum and providing photographic evidence to support them.

Children throughout the school are generally confident; they are problem solvers, independent in their exploring, they know how to behave and what aspects of the outdoor classroom may add to their learning. The children have learnt to work well in small groups and are able to support each other in most tasks, being confident enough to ask for support when they need it. The improvement in the children's personal and social skills is hard to measure, but becomes apparent when a new child comes from another school where they have not had the same consistent approach to outdoor learning. These new children are often more wary of the different environment and will usually struggle to be self occupying during their initial visits to the outdoor classroom; regular visits, though, support their transition into this new way of learning.

Some of the skills that the children develop in the outdoor classroom help support the learning that occurs when the children return to the main school and to their indoor lessons. There has been an improvement in playground behaviour with more tolerance and respect being shown by all children, and working in small groups has become less competitive and more supportive. Some teachers have noticed an improvement in children's observation skills and their concentration in the classroom; language and vocabulary has improved and enthusiasm for learning is obvious in the majority. The children at the school are very aware of their own environment and the impact that they can have on it; these skills are evident in the tidy school and well cared for green playground spaces.

In recent months the school has redeveloped its pond area and extended the perimeter fencing around the pond to ensure enough safe space to work with a whole class. The school effectively now has two outdoor classrooms, each with its own shelter and natural environment, extending the opportunities available and the number of children who can access the area at any given time.

Teachers are anticipating more visits to the outdoors, and in order for those visits to be learning experiences in all year groups they are currently writing a set of progressive skills to ensure age appropriate development in the future. The school is planning opportunities for children to spend time with their parents in the outdoor classroom, including camping experiences and storytelling alongside the already established workshops.

Now that the school has successfully incorporated outdoor learning into its everyday timetables and has planned and delivered successful lessons for many years, the challenge they now feel they face is maintaining its high priority. With staff changes and budget implications, year on year it will be important for a key member of the teaching staff to ensure that the use of the outdoor classroom remains stable. Teachers are also wary of the ever-changing curriculum guidelines and realize the impact this could have on their way of using the outdoors, so they work hard to make sure they are able to demonstrate learning in all sessions outdoors in order to justify its continuation into the future.

Case study: a large urban infant school

Forest School at Sedgemoor Manor Infants in Bridgwater has been running in its current form since 2000, funded originally with money from the Behaviour Improvement Partnership and more recently by Pupil Premium. The original funding allowed the school to recruit a full time Forest School leader to work across all year groups. At the start of the project there was very little money left over for equipment so the leader has needed to be resourceful in order to provide a variety of activities on a daily basis. These days the resources, mostly natural, are more plentiful and waterproofs are available for all children, with donated wellington boots ensuring children can remain dry on every visit.

Karen Staple, the Forest School leader, believes that extra resources are secondary to the outdoor space and the natural materials present. The creative use of space and new ideas has enabled the project to continue with the minimum fuss and allowed funding to be spent on waterproof clothing and other essentials. When Karen started at the school, due to a lack of space, she worked out of a collection of large bags, moving from class to class. She is now enjoying the luxury of some indoor storage and changing space for her frequent sessions. This, she believes, shows the impact of Forest School, highlighting the importance it has for the rest of the school.

Sedgemoor Manor is a large infant school in an industrial town in Somerset and, as with many town schools, it has a mixed catchment area, with a wide range of abilities, spoken languages and children with additional needs. It has the same problems as many schools and encouraging parents to take an active part in the school community is always challenging. However the school has a substantial turnout for its annual parents' sessions, with a noticeably high percentage of fathers attending the occasion. Forest School is also represented at the meeting for new reception families and an after-school club for parents has been successfully run in the past.

The school has one Level 3 trained leader, Karen, and a trained assistant and a member of teaching staff attends with each visiting group. Half a class visit the area at a time on a rolling programme, allowing for all children in the school to visit at least once a fortnight. There are additional sessions for small intervention groups, where an extra adult also attends. These intervention groups are generally kept very active and busy in order to prevent social problems and behaviour difficulties and Karen ensures there are a lot of opportunities for team building and social skills. These groups play a very active part in helping to develop their own learning space.

Karen has continually been changing and adapting her approach to planning and learning in the outdoor classroom, always striving to further improve the Forest School experience for the children. Although clearly a successful project, Karen feels there is always room to improve the integration of Forest School into the school curriculum and to make it indispensable. Her current focus is to consider how science can be taught through the Forest School sessions alongside the work going on in the classrooms. Having previously exposed the children to basic Forest School skills she is now looking for ways to incorporate this area, making it more meaningful for the learners. She shares her planning with all staff and is willing to adapt her style to suit individual classes, or indeed the child's individual needs.

Karen is seeking to find a new way to use individual target setting for the children visiting her from the nurture groups. If successful, she hopes this will help support the case for continued Forest School intervention and funding for the future. Karen and the other staff know that Forest School has become an integral part of provision in the school, supporting the creative curriculum and engaging all children in positive learning experiences. Karen is also willing to admit that her procedure for assessment is still evolving, working on getting the balance right between assessment, planning and preparation. With no nationally agreed Forest School curriculum and very few schools following this model, establishing the correct balance is a challenge.

There is little doubt in Karen's mind that Forest School has a significant impact on the children she works with and she has the full support of the headteacher and governing body. Some success can be seen very quickly, such as increase in confidence, self-esteem, interest in the great outdoors and some children are clearly more focused in all aspects of school life. Over time the school has seen significantly improved attitudes and social behaviour among its pupils.

Each year Karen looks for a new challenge. Last year it was the development of the school pond, this year it is building a plastic-bottle greenhouse. Where possible she encourages the school community to get involved, helping them to feel a sense of belonging and ownership.

Sessions are run every day and in all weathers. The length of a session is one and a half hours which includes changing time for the children. Generally, Forest School time consists of a set task where the children can complete the challenge in the way that they choose. There is some time for free play so the children can initiate their own learning ideas and then each session finishes with hot chocolate and a discussion about the visit and the tasks carried out.

The school has a range of environments which are used for Forest School. In the last few years willow sculptures and tunnels have been created and hazel hedgerows have been planted, ensuring a continuous supply of appropriate green sticks for cooking and generating kindling for fire lighting. The school pond is quickly becoming more established, there is a large school field, several wooded areas, planted beds and sensory areas. Storage is now provided by a large shed and additional space in the new Forest School room in the main building.

The school believes it is creating a model for Forest School that can be easily copied by others, and with several years experience behind them they are happy to share their expertise with other local schools, helping to keep outdoor learning high on the list of priorities.

Case study: nursery provision

The first Nature Kindergarten in Scotland was begun in 2006 in response to a need for full-time nursery care and in order to prevent the closure of an existing local setting. The founder and educational consultant Claire Warden spoke to local parents and built her new venture on the needs of these families and her own strongly held beliefs about how children should be cared for in their nursery environment. Claire has now created a sector-leading approach that has its own identity as a Nature Kindergarten, and as a testimony to its success the setting has been celebrated by Her Majesty's Inspectorate of Education (HMIE) for its quality of teaching and learning. Other countries have a range of other models also referred to as Nature Kindergartens, but this section of the chapter describes how this particular team have put multiple elements of successful education together to create their own outdoor learning approach.

After it was established, the setting immediately began using the outdoors as its main learning space, offering children up to six hours of outdoor play each day. The children have access to what is essentially a wild space, a nursery garden and the more traditional indoor learning space, creating three distinct learning areas, where uninterrupted play opportunities are nurtured, something that is not always as widely carried out as it should be in other settings.

Claire believes that the outdoors is essential to the children's development and well being and that the process of consultation with the stakeholders, in this case, the children and their parents, was essential for a purposeful project. She feels that the procedure she used to help design and integrate the spaces for learning was wholly appropriate and created the most effective learning experiences in the space available. The kindergartens make good connections with the children's families, providing community experiences and opportunities that encourage parental involvement and support. This helps parents to understand the experiences their children are receiving and, it is hoped, gives them the confidence to allow more wild and free play for their children in other areas of their lives.

The nursery's safe learning spaces and the adjoining traditional nursery buildings provide for children across the age range, replicating a traditional mixed age-group family set-up. This arrangement allows for the older children to become educators and role models for the younger children and for the younger children to aspire to be as able as their friends, and ultimately to be challenged by them.

Children have free-flow play between the areas of learning, and warm weather-proof clothing, provided by the nursery, ensures that the outdoor play is used throughout the year. Resources are, where possible, natural and it is important to the kindergartens that they are flexible and open ended. This, they believe, allows the children to have opportunities to be creative and use their imagination through their play, giving them the chance to play with the same things over and over, whilst always being able to alter what they are doing. In a more urban environment, where plastic cars and trains may be provided, the children often only play with those toys in one way. The Nature Kindergartens are attempting to give the children the chance to make their own games, each day making something different from the same pile of sticks and stones. These resources are preferably natural, gathered in the nursery grounds, and the intention is that they fully support the curriculum which has its foundations so strongly in the natural world.

The nurseries are acutely aware that using an outdoor wild space such as theirs comes with a range of potential unseen hazards for children. They are careful to provide experiences that allow the children to self assess the risk they are facing and make their own modifications to ensure their safety. The staff believe that children will not deliberately harm themselves and that the decisions children make about their capabilities are normally accurate and appropriate. Adults are there to support risky play, to remove unnecessary hazards, but to leave challenge and excitement in place. Children are encouraged to take part in activities that they may be wary of, but always at the level they choose for themselves. Through the continued support of carefully chosen, trained and supportive staff members and with encouragement these children learn to take a chance, attempt something new and recognize their own limitations.

Each area of activity is given a benefit-risk analysis by the nursery staff. They consider what the activity offers the children, how the children will learn and develop it and then they compare the positive outcomes to the risk involved. They take into account the needs of the children, their capabilities, confidence and their resilience in play and adventure. Staff are keen that, because one particular activity may be high risk to one child, it should not be restricted for others. Rather than limit the play the staff will adapt the activity accordingly, allowing all children to benefit from the experience, rather than none of them.

The children's ideas are respected and they are then guided on their own pathway through the curriculum. The staff here believe that the children do need to be involved in their own learning and in order to make their setting successful they have considered the environment from the perspective of a young child. Children are helped to engage fully in the three connected spaces within the nursery grounds: the indoors, the garden and the woodland. These particular kindergartens are internationally recognized for their work to provide this for the children in their care, and whilst other nurseries are keen to follow their lead, this group of kindergartens remains almost unique in its approach. Most others have free-flow play, outdoor areas, gardens and Forest School style experiences, but very few are able to offer such experiences all day, every day.

The powerful play environment is described by Claire as a wild space, with a carpet that renews each day and a ceiling of ever-changing light and colour. Such a play space is inspirational for children, encouraging creative play, descriptive language and a love for the world around them.

Summary

There is no doubt amongst the leaders and staff at each of these settings that their provision is greatly enhanced by the experiences children receive in the outdoors. There is a general opinion that the children have higher self-esteem and improved confidence, with practitioners noticing this over a series of sessions in the outdoors. It is agreed that children have the time and opportunity to practise their social skills, their physical skills and a chance to improve how they communicate with both their peers and the adults caring for them.

It is interesting to note that all three settings have provided time for parents to explore the provision and get involved in the learning experiences their children are a part of. All suggest that this has helped them to build an affinity with the outdoors and to develop their own confidence, not just that of their child. There is also agreement that involving parents greatly reduced their anxiety about the welfare and safety of their children.

These examples of good practice show how Forest School and similar experiences can be widely introduced across all areas of education. It is also apparent that it is not just the outdoor classroom and the extended school environment that allows for such experiences, but that enthusiastic, well-prepared and trained staff are an essential requirement to provide experiences that continue to be developed and modified for the very best opportunities for young children and their families.

6 | Conclusion

Throughout this book there has been discussion about the historic aspects of outdoor learning and comparisons made with the modern UK curriculum for children under the age of eight years old. As with all things historic, maybe outdoor learning is just a phase we are working through. It was important to Froebel working in the eighteenth century and again to Montessori and Steiner one hundred years later; now in the twenty-first century outdoor learning has again become an important and growing area of learning for young children. Perhaps as with fashion, outdoor classrooms will, at some point in the future, be replaced with a new trend and learning in the outdoors will no longer be a high priority.

In my opinion, outdoor play is more valuable that just a short-lived movement and research has shown that it has an impact on all areas of a child's development. The longer the outdoors is used and developed, the stronger the findings of new research will be, and the positive outcomes and reasons for its continuation will become more widely known among people working with young children. With research demonstrating there is a real need for this style of education I hope that future governments will consider making this aspect of education compulsory for all Early Years and Key Stage 1 children.

Outdoor play and learning is without doubt already imbedded in many early years' settings and reception classrooms. The challenge will be to give teachers of Key Stage 1 children the courage and confidence to develop this style of teaching in their classrooms. For this to happen, the outdoor classroom needs credibility and evolving evidence. It may also need a change in the attitude of people already practising outdoor learning. Forest School-trained staff believe in independent choice of activity, freedom to play, opportunities for collaborative working and thinking. These practitioners would probably frown on over-planned lessons, with set objectives and measurable success criteria. But such attitudes are not necessarily helping others to follow their lead. Maybe these confident and experienced practitioners are at risk of making their domain impossible for others to work in. Perhaps after 20 years of dictating how the outdoors should be used it is time there is a return to allowing people to plan and use the space in a way that they are comfortable with.

Using the outdoors at all, however planned and structured, is a step in the right direction. This way is likely to be how trained and experienced teachers feel most comfortable working. Many will need a lesson plan, objectives and a resource list in order to deliver these experiences. We should start to be more trusting of them, accepting that they will do the right thing for the children in their care; they will recognize the importance of the unplanned work going on and understand the need for children to stray from the directed lesson. Are well-qualified and experienced Forest School leaders in danger of preventing the programme of outdoor learning developing into Key Stage 1?

Staffing and attitudes to new practice are not the only problems faced by those trying to develop the use of outdoor learning. Through my own observations, it is apparent that money and resources are probably the two biggest problems facing school early in the twenty-first century. An increasing population means that school buildings are being pushed to their limits, with every nook and cranny being used for one-to-one work or small intervention groups. Temporary buildings, as the cheapest way of providing additional classroom space, are guilty of taking away areas of outdoor space to provide for more indoor learning. But as it has been for many decades, indoor learning is prioritized and resources for these new spaces are taking money away from the developing outdoors. Of course it is a requirement that class sizes cannot exceed a certain number of children, so maybe there is a need for additional building, but perhaps we should be trying to find a way of counteracting this development of the indoors. Maybe for each new building there should be a small coppice planted, or a new area for a school garden should be developed. Perhaps these new buildings, however temporary, should include doors into a safe outside area, a garden or a section of the playing field. Those of us working in schools are only too aware that there will never be enough money to create such a reality, so we should be looking for creative ways to fundraise and making strong links with the local community, where valuable help is often available. Many of the best outdoor learning spaces have depended upon money raised and donations of time and labour to get them started.

Let's not forget that this book is about the children and we should be encouraging their involvement from the outset. Children will know what they want to play with, what constitutes outdoor fun, and what they consider is risky is likely to be very different from our own interpretations. Children have creative ideas and will enjoy being involved in the planning of a new outdoor learning environment, and even the most experienced adult cannot see play through the eyes of a child.

Children will be less critical than adults and will use their imagination if the resources are sparse; they will create their own achievable expectations and will make their own challenges. Therefore, taking ideas from the children will make the play completely appropriate for their age and stage of development. For example, they will not consider the mud or the rain an inconvenience, rather another exciting element to their play. Using the children's own ideas creates a feeling of importance, makes a child feel respected and valued and adds to their feeling of self worth and importance.

The settings used to help collate the information for this book all demonstrate how children can be involved in the process of working and playing outdoors. Their ideas are put into place, explored and modified, adapted by the other children. Successful outdoor classrooms allow this collaborative approach, regardless of how thoroughly the sessions are planned. Some of these settings make clear links to the curriculum before the sessions; others add these links after the lesson has ended. Practitioners have to learn to do what is the right thing for them and their children. They must hold their heads high and know that they are allowing the children to have access to a full and enriching environment.

Whatever the space you have to work with I hope that you have been able to take an element of this book and use it to either continue or begin your teaching in the outdoor classroom. Take confidence from what you have read and be brave enough to try a new experience with the children in your care. They will be the judge as to its success.

Useful reading

Banks, J., Hamilton Shield, J. and Sharp, D. (2011) Barriers engaging families and GPs in childhood weight management strategies. *British Journal of General Practice*, August 2011 (http://www.rcgp.org.uk).

Bilton, H. (1999) *Outdoor Play in the Early Years*. David Fulton Publishers: London.

DfES (2006) *Learning Outside the Classroom Manifesto*. Crown Publications: Nottingham.

Edgington, M. (2004) *The Foundation Stage Teacher in Action*. Paul Chapman Publishing: London.

Fisher, J. (1999) *Starting from the Child*. Open University Press: Buckingham.

Green, J. (2010) *Learning Outside the Classroom*. LCP: Leamington Spa.

Green, S. (2011) *Outdoor Explorers*. Franklin Watts: London.

Harriman, H. (2006) *The Outdoor Classroom, A Place to Learn*. Corner To Learn: Swindon.

Hurst, V. and Joseph, J. (1998) *Supporting Early Learning: The Way Forward*. Open University Press: Buckingham.

Knight, S. (2009) *Forest Schools and Outdoor Learning in the Early Years*. Sage Publications: London.

Lindenfield, G. (1994) *Confident Children*. Thorsens: London.

Lindon, J. (1999) *Too Safe for Their Own Good*. The National Early Years Network: London.

Louis, S. (2009) *Knowledge and Understanding of the World in the Early Years Foundation Stage*. Routledge: Abingdon.

Macgilchrist, B., Myers, K. and Reed, J. (1997) *The Intelligent School*. Paul Chapman Publishing: London.

Nicol, J. (2010) *Bringing the Steiner Waldorf Approach to Your Early Years Practice*. Routledge: Abingdon.

Nurse, A. (2009) *Physical Development in the Early Years*. Routledge: Abingdon.

O'Brien, E. and Murray, R. (2006) *A Marvellous Opportunity for Children to Learn: A Participatory Evaluation of Forest School in England and Wales*. Forest Research: Farnham.

Rodger, R. (1999) *Planning an Appropriate Curriculum for the Under Fives*. David Fulton Publishers: London.

Ryder Richardson, G. (2008) *Creating a Space to Grow*. David Fulton Publishers: London.

Tovey, H. (2007) *Playing Outdoors*. Open University Press: Maidenhead.

Ward, J. (2008) *I Love Dirt*. Trumpeter: London.

Warden, C. (2010) *Nature Kindergartens*. Mindstretchers: Scotland.

Useful websites

Child of the Nineties:

http://www.bristol.ac.uk/alspac/documents/less-than-3-per-cent-take-enough-exercise.pdf

The National Primary Curriculum:

http://curriculum.qcda.gov.uk/primarycurriculum.aspx

Ideas and suggestions to help support Forest School work:

http://www.foresteducation.org

Forest Education Initiative (2005). *What is an FEI recognized Forest School?*:

http://www.foresteducation.org/forest_schools.php

Green Light Trust, a charity supporting learning in the outdoors:

http://www.greenlighttrust.org/

Mindstretchers, the home of Nature Kindergartens:

www.mindstretchers.co.uk

Ofsted support for early years care:

http://www.ofsted.gov.uk/early-years-and-childcare

Index